Midwinter Day

Also available from New Directions

A Bernadette Mayer Reader
Proper Name & Other Stories
Scarlet Tanager
Poetry State Forest

Midwinter Day

*

Bernadette Mayer

A NEW DIRECTIONS BOOK

Midwinter Day was originally published in 1982
by Turtle Island Foundation, Berkeley, California

Manufactured in the United States of America
First published as New Directions Paperbook 876 in 1999

Library of Congress Cataloging-in-Publication Data
Mayer, Bernadette.
Midwinter day / Bernadette Mayer.
p.   cm.
ISBN 978-0-8112-1406-3 (acid-free paper)
1. Winter – Massachusetts – Poetry.
2. Winter solstice – Poetry.
I. Title.
PS3563.A952M54   1999
811'.54–dc21   98-54649
CIP

New Directions Books are published for James Laughlin
by New Directions Publishing Corporation
80 Eighth Avenue, New York 10011

15 17 19 20 18 16 14

Midwinter Day

Stately you came to town in my opening dream
Lately you've been showing up alot
                                        I saw clearly
You were staying in the mirror with me
You walk in, the hills are green, I keep you warm
Placed in this cold country in a town of mountains
Replaced from that balmier city of yours near the sea
Now it's your turn to fall down from the love of my look
You stayed in the hotel called your daughter's arms
No wonder the mother's so forbidding, so hard to embrace
I only wait in the lobby, in the bar
                                I write
People say, "What is it?"
I ask if I must tell all the rest
For never, since I was born
And for no man or woman I've ever met,
I'll swear to that,
Have there been such dreams as I had today,
The 22nd day of December,

Which, as I can now remember,
I'll tell you all about, if I can
                                        Can I say what I saw
In sleep in dreams
And what dreams were before your returning arms
Took me like a memory to the room I always return to
When thought turns to memory's best love, I learn to
Deny desire from an acquired habit of vigilant fear
Till again to my nursed pleasure you and this love reappear
Like a story
Let me tell you what I saw, listen to me
You must be, you are the beginning of the day
When we are both asleep you waken me
I'm made of you, you must hear what I must say
                                        First I thought I saw

People all around me
Wondering what it is I write, I saw up close
The faces of animals, I slid down a long grassy hill
Past everyone doing everything, I was going faster
There were no streets to cross, no dignity lost,
A long story without pausing
I was racing, no one approved of what I was learning,
I saw a woman's daughter, we met on the stairs
I saw everything that was ever hidden or happening
I saw that my daughters were older than me
But I wanted to see further
                                        Nobody including you
Of all the people doing things, was approving
Of my sliding like this down the long tilting hill
Past the place to play and all the past
                                        I saw the moon's
Last quarter in the southern sky at dawn
                                        Then I saw
The shawls of the dream as if they were the sky
And the dream's dark vests and the dream's collar and cuffs
Of black leather on the dream's black leather jackets
I was alone in the dream's dressing room trying on

Different styles of tough gang-wear or raingear
In the dream my daughters Sophia and Marie
Are always with me
                              Then we climb
A mountain to the Metcalf's house, Nancy's fixing us
The eighteen intricate courses of a Japanese dinner
We sit at a counter curving around the kitchen
Like what they call a kidney-shaped pool
Eating hearts of heads of wet red and green lettuce
In the most high and palmy state of friendly love
Then Paul takes us all on a trip
                                        A while ago
The Japanese lady who lives next door smiled
When Marie smelled the fragrance of her cultivated rose
Sometimes dream is so rampant, so wild
As to seem more luxuriant than day's repose
So without riot spreading everywhere
How can I be both here and there?
                                        Then I found
A message in an over-sized book
On the way to Allen Ginsberg's nursery school
Where Ken Kesey was conducting a big picnic
                                        Then I saw
All the buildings of New York drawn to look
Like the illustrations in a children's book
                                        I dreamed
The road was so slippery from a truck's oil spill
We had to stop at a truckstop
Though our friends who were ahead of us might lose us
All the food in this place is served in a big dollhouse
And the salad's in a hatbox, they're catering to us
It's hilarious, suddenly we all crack up
                                        We say
You don't just eat from the desire to see a vine
Which today is called a chicken sandwich
You do seem to eat because you wear a hat and so
The hat's box is empty and must be filled with food

3

Do you see what I mean, it was a special restaurant
I was with Grace Murphy
                    Then I dreamed
I was ordering pompoms
Not those ornamental tufts on hats and not chrysanthemums
But a kind of rapid-firing machine gun
Really I can't figure out what's good and what's bad
I know I want to awaken feeling
Some remembered perfection
For which I crave a homeopathic dose of evil
Like the hair of the dog in the proverb
To offset the unsteady state of memory
                                    What man or woman
Could this be involving, so fleet it is indulging
In not quite flying but dreaming, flaunting
The short-lived continuity of a sound like hummingbirds
What is a story
            Can I say that here
Or should I wait till later wherever the question
Of life's chronology of satisfying the favored senses
Might better gratify the falling course of the grave day
As I must come closer to inevitably waking up
Like a dying man is dying spoiling the favor
You might grant me to extend this liberal time
And remit my punishment due though I've confessed already
And been forgiven
Are you going to convince me
There's nothing more to dream up
Like sins not committed but related anyway
To cover innocence
Always listening to everything you see,
Watching the sounds of the day
                            Wouldn't it be possible
To eat everything
All the collected foods even you
And one's self like the dinosaurs just dying out
In some unaccountable hungry fall, cunningly saintlike

4

                              The night cometh
When no man can work
And David saw that Saul was come out to seek his work
                                        I dream
I vault the fence, there's a cheerleader
Who needs to be kissed and caressed, it's like a blizzard,
Like my father I lost my color wheel when I died
I go vaulting over the consequent fence and with my ambition
I meet Gregory Peck
                    I always do
                              He looks like you
We go to the movies again, we go to two, we always do
And all the children are put,
Thrust, driven, goaded, impelled and flung,
Urged and pushed into bed
                              Then I can dream
We move again to the house where I was born
I'm wandering and forgetting, we are arranging
What rooms each of the children will finally sleep in
                    "Can Marie sleep in the hall bedroom
                    or is Andrew still alive?"
Andrew, who's like Bill
Or Bill's like him,
                    this state of things in dreams
                    could kill friendship if I told all
                    even to Uncle Andrew
                    who's also alot like Clark
Anyway I know we must share this copied house
With my grandfather, another Andrew, who is a little mean
Now everybody's here in this room and we are a party to death
I look at the old uncle who is still young Andrew or Bill
I am trying to remember where in time I am
I study his face but all I see is plain expression
Not the look of a man who's dead and knows it
Like something or someone nobody absolutely needs to know
I decide not to say anything about it
Already I've looked closer without moving to him,

5

A man without responses but that's beyond all this,
I say to myself in dream it's all the same
All the people in this room will surely die some time
Who cares which ones are already dead, I'm just here now
In my dream like I always am among the charms
Of sweet Andrew, charming Bill, I can't go on
                                        Is there an end

To such love and the duty of dreaming,
Things seen eyes closed not seeming to be dreams
Like the blackest edges once I saw outlining
Each leaf in spring one year or the jewels I saw
With Grace lying together before a thunderstorm
I could suggest to her then and she to me
What kind of thing would appear to us next
In the train of the vision moving from right to left
Under love's closed eyes
                          I hope you can see as much
When I try to suggest among lines of the evaporating word
What idea I've seen, what image each dream heard
There's no end to a narration of forms
From all the ways of looking eyes closed
                                      Now I see

What's ordinary like a sky
Or weather I can hear without ever looking
As blind people suddenly given sight
Sometimes will abhor it and shut their eyes again
To be more conversant with the actual view
                                        And I know

You too can see better in the dark
Love's eyes open anyway behind your quiet shoulder
I dream you awaken and it's day
I wish for the night of our reassuring love
Daily taken to the market and all kinds of stores
To be ridiculed and fooled, ignored and reduced
Daily tested by the tedium of uncondensed routine
Long mornings and lightless afternoons that exist in time
Till the night for both our work and love

Makes us feel love is the same
                              Before we had children
We used to work all night, eyes open, then sleep
For the day, eyes closed to people's mornings
                                          If we could
We'd walk out independent seeing everything so benefitting
Us, the sun and moving, then sleeping
Among our bright love, the path of the sun becoming
A modest warning of something we were studying
                                        Now that our days

Are full of normal parts
It seems we have all lived forever so far
Eyes open, eyes closed, half-open, one eye open
One closed to the coming day, past's insistence,
Dream's vivid presence, no one knows why
Though you can see all I say with half an eye
I always have an eye to fascination, you catch my eye
                                          This meditation

Not on sleep but on awakening
With dreams with everything quickening, you and I
Survive this work and rest, not so much lost,
We only seem to dream as quickly as we live
One for the other to make up time
                                    And it's as if

Today I had someone else's dreams
Everything's the reverse of what it seems
Alone at last, I'm also with you
The weather's fine, the sky's not only blue
                                  Like long preludes
I dream I don't want to get into this
But it's soothing and exciting like weathering
This desire for you, you are being blown maybe away
Maybe from me by two men maybe they're women
                                        I don't know

At Ted and Alice's house, it's like love
I was mad, I was jealous, it was like love
                                    It must be
That dreaming has its effect on dreams

7

                                    Lying on a bed
In the dream Ted is on the phone like the Thomas Edison,
Tom, Ed or even John Thomas or the anonymous electrician
That he is he said and Alice said it's silly to be dead
Or jealous either but I feel mute, dumb and mad
And thus alive to those two women or are they men
Who are giving you a blowjob or at least repairing you
Which has to do with something Alice said and something
Bill said about the dangers of another
                                    The other is two
Is this a clue to wake up from dreams
And see what I'm forgetting?
                         Then a woman
I was watching was laid
                    Forgive me
On a table for something medical to be done
Like the glimpse of a scene I innocently noticed
In a movie on t.v.
                    God please let me
Be released
Like all songs' version of all loss of love
From the movie version of any of my memories
Let me go,
            "Incident in San Francisco,"
                                    let me be
I've seen all this before just as innocently
Do I have to add
That in this sense I'm an incestuous guilty whore
Please love me anyway even if I dream my blood
Must be exchanged for the blood of another relation
Before your eyes made new like my old reputation
Something was introduced into the system or taken,
An operation, no clearer to me than I've made it to you,
                                          Sorry,
That's how it was, I was watching a woman
And something was being done to her tentatively
Then recovered we sat down together to eat

A large flat dull dry cake like awful life
I broke it into pieces in my adolescent plate
                                    Mothers and fathers
Beware of these bereft dream cakes
Not like Nancy's mother's milk potato pancakes
But dry and without salt and fat preserving life
Desultory and unleavened like communion
As pleasant to taste as the host eaten at a funeral Mass
I do take in this sado-masochistic ceremony
Obviously not medical but
Cannibalistically sexual, primal and hereditary
                                    It reminds me
Of Marie's fascination with watching
Sophia's response to pain
And in this revolting sextet of dreams
Where there are two of everyone in every scene
I am watching and hungry to wait
While something's done to someone
                          Not me or Bill or Nancy or Andrew
But Lewis who, if I need him
Can stand in in dreams for my entire past
                                    Not to speak of
His love for Bill and Bill's for him, Nancy's mothering,
My love for that pleasure, for her,
Paul and Bill and Lewis and all their parents,
Formidable Adrian, not Paul and Nancy's daughter of that name
But another one who's dark
                          The dream's not exactly fair
Their other daughter's name is Ann, Nancy's had two girls,
So have I, so did my mother and Beverly, that's Bill's wife
There are two Bills
                          And so to take a breath
If Bill and Paul (and Lewis) could be fathers to me
Because each is a man who has had two daughters
Then they could also be
The two men in the dream who became two women
Must I go on?

9

Ted and Alice have two boys
And Ted could be short for Theodore, my father's name
So even if the two men were Ted and Alice's two sons
It's clear the women they became were my two daughters
Seducing their father
                    Do you see what I mean?
No wonder I was so mad
And that's why the woman had to have an operation
                                        Bill said

An old Greek woman he used to pass on the street
Saw him with his two daughters and said
"A big man like you! Why not produce sons!"
                                    If Lewis
Is my father and my daughter is my mother
After whom she's named
                        Then all this confusion in the dream
Legitimizes the scene and it is not incest
                                    First girls
As infants love their mothers who are women, then girls
Learn how to love men unless they become homosexuals;
Boys love their mothers first too and can continue
To love women when they grow up
Unless they're homosexuals
                            The mothers of men and women
Are always being loved more later by sons
Than by daughters who seem to love fathers better
Because that's the way it is
                        They say
Women love later in a more complicated way
Than men who never had to learn to change
                                    The sex
Of what they call the love object
Though they might have anyway
                                There's more to it than that
Like a woman's identification with a hat or the ground
Or a man's with cars, wars or the other way around

                                        Bill said
His brother belongs to the Hare Krishnas
Who only want to have sons, not daughters
Like the old idea of throwing them in the river
This dream unnerved me
Famous Lewis isn't Theodore, gift of God, nor is Ted
I'm not Marie Ann Bernadette
I'm Bernadette Frances Catherine
My daughter has a teddy bear
                                Fuck this shit!
Let's get on with it, let's die of fucking respect
This respectable mourning is fucking forbidden
Day's desirable plans are dressed like dreams
Which sell the whole of what I already bought once
Back to me, night's deal, to become a part
Of day's dalliance with the logic of dream's art
                                        I'd like to open

A stationery store
In a small New England town, it'd be called
The Scarlet Letter
                        I dream I'm Lillian Hellman
Meeting Jane Fonda
                        I don't know why, as far as I know
Lewis' Aunt Julia is fine, perhaps it's because Heather,
A name like Pearl, is the name of the printer's daughter
And his business is called the Hawthorne Press
                                        Which reminds me
Of another dream about a luncheonette
Like this random rhyming this joint was Puerto Rican
And like Mike's Variety which used to sell stationery
In this narrow town, it was a long narrow place
Kind of what you might call a hole in the wall
                                        In the dream
We live upstairs like the local grocer Reno Cimini
Who reminds me of the Borgia's or a burgher
Running a place you can run down to for coffee to go

                                        In the dream
They served hot spiced jelly at a clean white counter
The jelly's on a lazy Susan, I feel I'm on vacation
                                        Keith Thompson,
Heather's father, is behind the counter
Saying how hard it is to run a small business
Just like Hawthorne, he says, who ran a bookstore
Combined with a pepper mill, as we all know
                                        Maybe it was called
The Scarlet Letter in the dream, I can't remember
                                        It's night
I stay a long time, then you
Come limping and staggering down the street
Lewis, why are you so old and so sick?
                                        Then I see
It's not you at all, it's only my mother
                                        And once again
I help you down the street, you're complaining
I remember you're interrupting all my fun
                                        Dear Lewis,
When I imagine something's wrong with me
I immediately attribute this weakness to you
And in this way I make you stand in for my mother
As I'm sure most people who live together secretly do
I do apologize, I know you are completely another
                                        Then Bob Callahan
Pretending to be Don Byrd
Came to snap our picture and we felt he might steal our souls
He had a craggy old face like the detective
In Nicolas Freeling's books, Henri Castang
I looked at Bob's face while he posed us
He said you must hold still for two whole minutes
The camera starts buzzing and clicking by itself
Like a time exposure gone haywire except you could see inside
To the shutter and the lens like a lentil,
All the secret future
                                        Then I said
Please only do our profiles, it's much too long to look

And that's when someone brought in my old broken trunk
We were going to use it but I guess Marie broke it
And the whole inside or lining of the trunk was coming out
I think to myself I guess that's my body
And this means I'm dreaming isolation is more healthy
Than having a family
Saying this seemed to make sense
                              Then I said
I guess it's really broken and cannot be repaired at all
And that's the end
                    How suggestible
As in a dream of leaves under fluorescent lighting,
Next I dream I am imitating your handwriting
                                    These dreams are like
Arithmetic by Plato, I can count and figure the shadow
Of each mother, daughter, father, each representative
                                          I dream
A strong brown woman not a black woman but a woman
Named Brown who stands for a rich motherly woman
Has us to her house for a party
It's a house like an institution with a gymnasium
                                    Then Cadillacs
And big Lincolns and Mercedes Benz's
All line up by the side of the road for an assassination
There's a meeting of men
All the sons of the people of the world at the party
                                        And suddenly
Men on motorcycles come and assassinate all of them
We're standing directly in the dream's line of fire,
Sophia, Marie and I, but we don't get hit
                              Then we
Have to tell the woman her son is dead, shot
By a gang of assassins, there's a complication,
She doesn't seem to notice us
                          The party's moved
To an indoor swimming pool like in "Alphaville"
Where people dive into the water while they're being shot at

She says, "It's a happy occasion today" and we all say
She must be a strong woman to deal in such a way
With the death of her only son
                          The way daughters-in-law
In books murder the rich mothers of their husbands
To steal money and property and love away from them
Like in *Sabine* where an old woman poet is murdered
Because of her house
                          This is the mathematics
I'm the mother and the poet
Something is inferred about an artist who died
The daughters are intact, the dream-sons are murdered
What's the equation
When the mother of the fear of daughters
Is the artist not the patroness of double sons,
Has she lost less?
                          Is she the opposite of strong?
They say it's a happy occasion when a baby's born
They say about the weather, what we curse we bless
The rich woman now stands for the mother
And the only son who died is the father
I can't continue with this
                          Then Gregory Peck
Sat in the front seat of the car and kissed his girlfriend,
She was only ten or eleven years old, he reminds me of you,
We were at another party and he was on the phone to Hollywood,
Who are the sons of Solomon?
                          I denigrated the wine
As being too sweet, then the maid pointed out
Each bottle still had a price label,
                          $26.75
How prodigal all these rich people are like the trees
I tried to find a way to get free of the indulgent rigidity
Which made me resent good wine in a dream
                          I poured some more
But the room was so crowded the glass overflowed
                          Then we went to sleep

14

And I fell from my innocent bed almost in time
To be caressed by a desirous Gregory Peck, you again,
Who used to be my mother's favorite actor,
"The Man in the Grey Flannel Suit"
                              Why do the boys shout
On the small-town street at night and crave the speed of cars,
There's a girl who used to stand on the corner in the middle of town
All day or sit across the street on the town's park bench
Waiting, I imagine, to score something, the arithmetic
Is too personal but fathers do have daughters
If they don't have sons and Matthew Tannenbaum
Whose name means Christmas tree in German has a snapshot
Of a twelve-year-old girl on his desk
                              In the dream
I get a quick casual kiss from Mr. Gregory Peck
Though I'm falling out of bed from desire for his prick
I seem to be dreaming about all the rich mothers I know
Who, in an image, might lose their sons in wars
While traditionally daughters give their fathers pleasure
In the idiosyncratic case of my dream obsessively
Mathematically subtracting from the pleasure of the mother
Of daughters whose husbands will inevitably want to murder her
While the father's in bed with the daughters
                                        Then won't the sons-
In-law want to murder *him*?
                              I've gone off the deep end
Dreams like obsessions are a relief not to think about
It's all counting and figuring wrong like arithmetic lists
Rich American people seethe within big cars, expand without
Ever breaking the unaesthetic table with their frenetic fists
The best dreams are free stories like a present of food
I want to have a big dream about only leaves
Or a place I've never seen which interweaves
Not with the old subtracted love of which I am bereft
But the unequalled new, what I can't count, with which I'm left
                                                  I saw
Another dream plane and a mechanical horse

So complicated I woke up before I could get on it

                                        I was reminded
Of finding out from dreams what a story is
I was strongly invited to remember as an ember
That the ferries terrified us inwardly
Even Peter hated me, I had to take the blame
For being in a house without fortunes or beer
In a flat sandy town around the corner
From the mountains at the beach
We swam the channel in lanes
But the ferries terrified us

                        An old man, a transient,
Needed a cheap peaceful place to stay
For a few days, he couldn't get the words out
I listen being patient because I'm also old
And I've learned to sit up straight
We lost all our money speculating in beer
Manufactured like company matchbooks
I was in alot of places like policemen go to
I explained all this

                        People, animals and plants
Do what they do today again tomorrow
This is something I can't say about you
It follows that children take a long time to grow
We speed it up but everything is slow

                                Like the Straits of Gibraltar
Before I was being at the understood place
Existing or happening now
I guess I was in process and in contrast
With past, future past and future

                                Today I'm the present writer
At the present time the snow has come
At this moment we won't starve
At once the ferries terrify us and
We knead red and green peppers with
Our contrasting hands

16

                    At a time
Very close to the present I want to get
A tight pair of pants and dance
With you with things as they are
                              Now and then
Just talking to talk or reading to read
And exchanging great reading with others
Someone says don't say sleep tight
And don't let the bedbugs bite
                         Now we'll never know
If the dough I was kneading
Was play-doh or cash, I don't do you?
Just now people need Christmas money
Sweet thick-skinned red and green peppers
Gimme yours, nowadays that's not funny
Now and again I always need you
Don't be absurd, go back to sleep
                              Come now
It's Midwinter Day today a day
To cause the sun to stand still as it will anyway
At a point on its ecliptic furthest away
And from now on, they say, things will turn our way
To me the sun complains of such a phony culmination
The Great mistaken Circle of the Celestial Sphere,
Sun's apparent annual path, man's mere erudition,
Old egocentric notions of who is who and what is where
                                             Here
Winter makes us wet and cold and old
Like a man of eighty winters who will keep
Hot food on the rickety stove like stories told
To pass midwinter night and never sleep
                              It's December
It's the dead of winter, remember
Sun setting red on the hill of red trees
Cold dusk's blue clouds white skies
I count the days
               I dream

"It's o.k." So much stuff in dreams
Seems to come from books it's as if
The sun does revolve around the earth
And everyone is writing about you,
All the authors are my neighbors
And everyone is still living in a restaurant
On Madison Street in a trash-novel locale
In Ridgewood, Brooklyn, Queens, New York
                                        Where I grew up
My mother never drank no liquor at all
Just an occasional social highball
                            Morning mist, grasshoppers,
I read everything upside down,
Who can I trust to hold the babies now?
                                    I follow the map,
I can't remember last September, words please be quiet
These ideas are like beans and peas
                                Warsh upstairs
Below, a behaviorist, next door a Porsche
Everyone puts up a sign with a name on it
Don't malign others so my mother might say
I never know what she might say
                            She won't go away
We all hear voices if we talk during the day
Can we trust words to hold the babies now?
Every day's a holyday of obligation ends
Speeding jets to jetports is now allowed
                                    I'm getting old
Or even thought beneficent, deemed efficient
Like a voguish mis-spelling
                        Hurry hurry
Get your penultimate forbidden Sundae
Or else your mother tells me people still dress up
For some occasions, I try to give the reading
But I miss the words because my poem is a map
                                    Marie,
There are just no words in this book, only pictures

I stumble for love while whispering to cover
Yet another version of *Pilgrim's Progress* I've cooked up
To dress my thoughts more primly, to grimly undress
Myself I drink more big bottles of obsessive beer

                                            Busch beer
Or Butch beer, it's mother's milk, Bitch beer
Sweet sugar milk, it's Touch beer

                            German Bush Tribesmen's beer
Beer left for me by my loud and thoughtful students
I'm still whispering or is it forgetting

                           All the words
Just the names of some heroes and heroines of the past
To whom I thought I could safely entrust
The babies' mysteries

                  Who is Constance?

                            Freud Pound & Joyce
Are fine-feathered youth's fair-weather friends
I take that back, better not to mention them
Or it's the end

               In my childhood house's hall
She is a feather and I am a mother
There's no real words on paper, that's all
And if I seem to write them I'm another

                       Then came
The movie stars, this fatherweight
I was told to go rest up
In a whorehouse for a while
Then go and think but not like a train

                       Where to put the penis,
Sophia's vagina bit a boy but
It was both ways, he actually bit her a bit
She couldn't understand why he put his finger in it
Then she said maybe you'd want this brown paper bag
Marie put her foot in the Mothercare catalogue
The rain it's raining on Charlotte Corday
Winter's coming in
The doorway of the foul Bombay subway

And on the ships at sea in Spain

                    Child's Garden of Verses

Worse things could happen
You could've married me and I'd turn out to be
Ava Gardner, then you'd see a double murder

                              David said

You see I'm a half-poet in a child's detective coat
My instinct is to sleep in your old or that man's
Cellar

        You see I'm man-woman or boy-girl at once
A car starts up to find us out hiding

                         You say

Let's move the pillows so the driver won't see
He shows us his wardrobe in a wardrobe

                              He says

You see I had to move to this cellar
So nobody would steal my check shirts

                         You and I

Walked away from the table
But the street as home was dismal
In this stumbling child's life
Poetry's

        Crowded all up again in anybody's roomy car
Fucking up the gears of any day

                    You say

His or her highness is iterating something, splendid,
You owe world living so world is owing you

                              I dream

Everyone is doing something like delivering sun
I get nearer to the face of the moon

                         Someone says

I wanted to see Grand Central one more time
Before you remind me again death like everything
I had tried to foresee couldn't have been any other way
I love the bending window

                    I dream

It's a sandwich but the bread is the meat

Your echoic lips dispel the pretty dream scene
I ask you then for toys and quick machines
And Romanesque and Grecian westerns with lions,
This eats this better than this
                              I dream
The dull moon's rehearsal for a day is a leaf
Spread like muffins with butter from the trees
I just ate 30 of them or 31 or 32 or 33
Or thirty-four soon my life is at least half over
Yet your secret lover still asleep
Must fear the world's displeasure as of a mother
If she dreams of a man at whom a pie was thrown
If she dreams of awakening alone
                                        It's the Annunciation again
I hate the dreadful patience of all these saints
These cold stunned flies can't even move
Lying casually covered in pain everywhere near
My bitten neck, my drafty desk, my lesbian pencil
And so they bite me, winter flies, they can't die
                                        As quick as I
Rush to the window to know the time of day
And what's across the street to meet us when we wake
I'm impatient with excitement to invite you
To share what can't be seen
                              Every morning I think
I've become the new weather
Like embroidering something after, trying to remember
The half-lies of dreams
                       A day halfway
Between fall and spring
To which I bring
The past will rest exchanged
And forgetting but for you
To whom I turn to sing

From the vigil sleep has kept we'll arise
Hopefully with vigor like an unwise plant

We'll come to our senses excited and lively
Like a watch kept on the eve of a festival
My devotions are held by such an eye to you

If I'm going to die I think I'll paint your portrait formally to make us
feel important in a style filled with messages and learned as if
we're famous, I wonder what I see
Children cry at everything, they don't know logic like a habit you
hide though another admires it, your bent for secretiveness or
mystery, gratuitous benefits like if humans could fly
I still think sheep for sleep not being learned yet at all, not only did
Stein write at night but for mornings she's forbidden remem-
bering, I remembered to put out a new pencil for myself,
otherwise, sweet Shakespeare, I did want more
Sense of senseless helplessness if fear's not reformed like a Catholic
before he can begin again again, better for her to forget it,
what was it
I said nothing I said surely I would have to change from being this
drunken unreformed sybarite to being a more sober mother,
it was nothing forbidden just fruit for more sleep the way
sleep can also be ideal
Hawthorne never wasted paper, his hand so cramped by the Berk-
shire weather he fit more words in, remember when William
Shirer put cherry gelatin in my drink in the dream and then
the mail truck came to his studio and lurched and pinned me
down, I was involved in creating a soup with pickles in it, it
was the perfect soup, there's no end to these dreams, if only I
could remember to solve problems, what does hot pickles
connote
I dream with the streetlight on my face if only loss were less exotic,
what time is it, I used to feel one way as a child awakening
and do they, once went on forever, now athletic in the seasons
like poetry, I'm refusing to understand what I mean
But you're doing some kind of moving too, insensate concatenations
of two minds banging things in bed, bed's a solid word,
what's this lethargy in limbs, I don't stop to prove I'm not so
old, now I'm somewhat old, the winter is old

We dream we yell making unheard-of-noises, it's sweet to wake to
      some extent, I wonder what we'll be like when we're really
      old, some old people live on one can of soup a day, the soup
      of too much thought seems to be making us rusty and hungry
I remember dreaded childhood wakenings in the ice-cold room
      wondering if there's time to put laid-out clothes under covers
      to warm them before rush to dress sometimes forgetting
      some of the underwear, grandfather wouldn't waste heat,
      they shovelled coal into a furnace, the room was still a dark
      one, these pillows are walking away with my affections, wak-
      ing in Great Barrington almost perfectly in the path of the ris-
      ing sun so as never to miss anything, going to sleep there
      alone in the dark silent isolated house with so many secret
      rooms, not my house
Usually there are dreams of the unexpected secret extra room down a
      hallway which extends the house into the world, this room
      happens to be red white and blue, I wonder what are some new
      things to drink, breathing love, do I deprive you of anything?
Tea's always something to drink, Ted once said cheese wasn't food, a
      long day in which to reform all this adoring to something,
      what is it, it's bad enough in midwinter if nothing else hap-
      pens, I might get used to becoming you and no one would
      think that was good, then I'd feel lost as a simple body
We are not going to exactly the same tasks every day and beginning
      with warm feet, you are too nervous anyway, we repeat alot
      because of the children which I can't get used to saying, they
      don't know logic at all, it's o.k. to say kids but when someone
      says the kid I don't like it
Small babies or infants are supposed in the mythology to be women's
      penises, I meant to say psychology, Marie would like to have
      one so she puts a shirt or a ruler between her legs, I think she
      thinks about her diaper as a penis and so she doesn't want to
      lose it, Mabel said we forget how comfortable they are
What did I ever lose anyway, not a hair of her head, here's my license,
      I never used it, like your father's diplomas, he's a lawyer and a
      real estate agent but he never practiced, what an asinine use of
      the word, either of them, like the pencil in my dream

I wonder if Ted is still in the electrician's union, is it wrong to steal
rightly just like memory who needs it badly, an affectation
like a scarf called worn jauntily or the noise of the buttons on
my cuffs brushing the bed in time to a rhyme, Marie hears
every noise the same, she doesn't not hear anything

The bed is like a typewriter, sometimes I think the bed's a refrigera-
tor with the holographic head of a man in dichroic color to be
seen in ambient light on the door, I mean the cover of the
book the bed is, you do look all the time at some of the same
things until the names of objects might as well fall off

Then maybe you die, that's the scare of mornings, it's loose or lush
like this or blood but darker than it ought to be, it all has a
beauty and a structure I haven't seen all of yet like a story, I
always forget the most important part

Go back black to sleep's gray, who'd ever read it anyway, only the
ones who already know me, it's no great mystery at this rate
history might pass us by as a group of unrelated people or-
dered out of the same house, we could be better poets just on
the phone

I better hurry to accommodate family to see what's going to happen
with them today, every morning's the same dawning before
it's talked about or told like the dull man who wanted to tell
the dream he had of you a week ago, then he never said it, he
just said it was recurrent

Doesn't everybody know everything or not, please let me know,
isn't the truth always the same, firm as a tree, is it an accident
or pose that I say what I say, can I look into the dream room
and then run away?

Then I'll tell you how each day is different, a tree it's true can be
thought to be you, I don't know logic either, babies are as if
insane

Doesn't something, whatever it is, seem so diagrammed not like a
sentence, not like turning over to have another dream, but the
consequent rest, what I mean is once life begins it has a stasis
or a balance or a standing that is what it is, it's not mechanical,
what's strange is this

Eyes, windows, children, words, even the seasons not to speak of
        feelings, sleep is ship's gray, deck paint put on the floor of an
        immobile house, this ship's deck of cards is spilling into the
        ocean unwittingly
I can't remember any more, I have to see something new like a model
        or a star so concerned with the figure of sun before air through
        the window like a page near the invented bed we share in a
        room we rent for shelter from the elements as I am to speak
And I look out
                There's no fiction in it
The supplicating weather is either this or that
                                        Today it's
That saintly gray so far, there's nothing to it
Sleep is so morose, so loose and slack
To slip and sink in something like a lapse
Of something natural and regularly recurring
In a condition of lack of what we call conscious
                                        Thought,
Sensation, movement, even love
                        Just like death I slept
Now I know enough to ask what do you hear
When I listen?
                This morning I have both
A heart exchanging a guilty love for everyone
For love is the same
And you
                What is your substance and whereof are you made
                That millions of strange shadows on you tend?
                Since everyone has, every one, one shade,
                And you but one, can every shadow lend
There's something
I want to say, I don't know how to put it
                                Brightest Sun that dies today
                                Lives again as blithe tomorrow
                                But if we dark sons of sorrow
                                Set, O then, how long a night
                                Shuts the eyes of our short light

Don't take what I say too seriously
Or too lightly,
                    I'm sorry,
                              Nevermind
I was just playing around, I'm trying to find
What I guess I'd rather not know consciously
                              I'd like to know
What kind of person I must be to be a poet
I seem to wish to be you
                    Love is the same and does not keep that name
                    I keep that name and I am not the same
You,
Shakespeare, Edwin Denby and others, Catullus,
I've nothing else to say, the anonymous
Blue sky is gray, I love your being
In my unresisting picture, all love seen
All said is dented love's saluted image
In the ending morning, nothing said is mean,
Perhaps it's too long, I'm only learning
Along with love's warning
To invent a song
                    Then for the breath of words respect
                    Me for my dumb thoughts, speaking in effect
This was my dream
Now it is done.

· PART TWO ·

Sophia likes a cup of coffee to be in the picture too, she will climb the old trunk to the cold window without you in the room and then fall off while Marie is pretending to be me, you are wondering what it is you're doing.

I pick her up, you are pouring oatmeal into the measuring cup, there's a chipmunk singing in time to his tail in the honey locust tree where the cat was treed and a black bear in Windsor ran into the car of a man going west on Route 9.

On eggs or ordinary toothpaste, fantastic pigeons who always live above us murmuring fly, it looks like right at us, but hit the roof to rest where there's a space between the bricks before they fly out again, one is all white. That cat and a skunk are always in the yard.

Black tin cup made out of town of mountains of sky, the so-called true horizon parallel to the sensible, once I used to keep a flying squirrel as a kind of pet, the squirrel left the house in spring, the boundary of your favorite cup. There's jelly on *Borrowed Feathers*.

I say that chipmunk who can speak is learning to speak as you say you want to read a book which means look at it so you demand of me, say it. Delicate tantrums in tints and shades of the same corner you like an aversion to memory's rudeness in the form of what we call voices. You are being too loud.

If everything could happen at once even as merely as only two babies crying and requiring everything but nothing at one time, the desire to control something as small as any destiny begins to seem like just will. Or what world doesn't have religion to pass us off as ruling if not by law then in the morning at least for a while we're only thinking of ourselves.

My absorption in your clothes is only sensible, why bother to toast the bread but I'm willing, it's to make the bread warm, here's a royal blue shirt and red pants put into the words of your eyes not as dark as mine but darker than his whose eyes are impatient for a moment to see more than that you still need so much to be done in detail for you we can never seem to get out of the house.

Winter flies are dying by the windows, we are never without at least one as if we still know nothing just passing the time because we can't seem to finish, they repeat after me a mood like you shout moon or mom as loud as you can, it's all the same, you and I are like two transparent wings.

The person and the people are these mouth-size toys, broken Mother Goose Jack-in-the-box with Old King Cole on it clutters the hall with proper nouns like Donald Duck orange juice and Mickey Mouse Halloween masks, a real cow that milks, you say no look and oh first though other noises came once before to be better as sounds than nouns as memory or more than one of those like these clutters which are made of all this in all the rooms today which will be cleared and then will have been a mess like a person I'm fond of who's changed, not like a diaper.

Look at this, see, you do, which one are you. The book is said to be a duck. The color wheel reflecting you hiding, the bus, empty green swing for people, smiling tiger nothingness puzzle, empty-eyed monkey mask right there, battered stolen musical egg, look, bright old playgroup radio playing raindrops and so on, there's something about a thermometer you wouldn't understand yet, silly identical grounded queen bees, you put things into things now, you empty cups and trucks on your own articulating oh and no the same, grabbing for the fifteenth-century Dutch woman who looks chiding, that's why I put her up, that polar bear won't go into that nesting cup.

The potato masher in Marie's bed's as good to eat as prone Cadillacs I might want to give friends if I could if they were given to that, you're conversing, sudden kisses make you try to bounce without getting hurt by it but then hurt anyway by my observation come as a distraction you fall and get tired and since I'm anxious to be done I entertain the theory you've already forgotten for putting more of this into that and begin to take the first steps.

Divided in the light a length of day is measured more in numberless meals. Each of two children needs to be offered two breakfasts but the tone of this tradition seems to mean today one of you needs more to eat nothing, she just isn't hungry, at least not yet, grandmothers and books will say they have days like that, other mothers also do not wittingly give salt, how many eggs could be bad for you if you're only one, or three like a bad one not that anyone should use the word bad right away, you say do you think she hates her bib or is she finished, some foods are tokens like the cold round cereals once in the bowl, at least she's stopped standing up, now tell her again to

please sit down, the trees are getting cold, you wear a band of red
velvet before the old kind of milk standing sentry in between two
daughters, did you feed the fish.

Hold still the short light is old already, everything for you is momen-
tary, you may even whistle for a week or so, we've rearranged the
day again into another formal order, I'm hungry at the wrong times
like you but I can't remember to stop to eat because you like the light
are almost done, formidable ordinary order to present the day with
at least a little concentration on fierce love working like slowly build-
ing a house only adding to it in the seasons when there's extra time,
more for that than this continuous keeping us warm which the fin-
ished house will eventually do if only we had time to raise the roof.

I did put the rest of the clothes away though I did and didn't want to
in straight regular rows in an arrangement of peace among a series of
thoughts of the chaotic rank and still position of ourselves and where
we fit in the system of the news of the day, a portion of which was
submitted to the typesetters last night while we were sleeping and
planned and laid out on the big pages in order of importance which
begins in the upper right hand corner where the eye goes first, the
rest is editorials and speculation, some sensation but no color to hide
or uncover feelings like the mountains and so on better reflect. Old
Harry is another name for Satan.

From the bedroom, curtains blue as ink I stare at, red Godard floor
white walls all crayoned, from the bed raised on cinder blocks at Dr.
Incao's midwife's request so Sophia could be born, fake Indian cover
Ray gave us for Marie American Indian and Ray's old real wool
blanket and all our sheets her gifts, Lewis' Aunt Fanny's crocheted
afghan and Tom's old sleeping bag, the mimeograph machine and its
cover, diaper rash ointment, from the walls a butterfly kite, a leaf on
a ribbon from nursery school, mushrooms by Joe, an iris and a glad-
iola by Rosemary, the gladiola painted here, the stuck clock, the
window faces south, laundry on it, closet doors hung with jackets,

shawls, scarves and Marie's dress, closet floor boots shoes boxes bags baby carriers and my broken inherited chair, that's the airport, closet of stuff, carpet sweeper, another broken chair, from there I go to the kitchen sink you can sit on at the imagined forest window, two coleus plants too cold today, now a Wandering Jew, two related spider plants one is hanging, stones dead branches and collected pine cones, an old ghost and a Boston fern on the spooky refrigerator in which is the food, drawings of attempted faces by Marie that look like Cy Twombly, the dumb electric stove, George's red shirt calendar, soon it'll be over, the Lenox Savings Bank historical calendar, Pilgrims landed yesterday, winter begins today, shortest day of the year, Lewis and Harris with Marie in a Bronx corridor, little light, the African woman backpacking a baby, she's talking to a totem figure, a street scene by Raphael and a German altarpiece Rosemary sent, a crude drawing of a nude woman by Paul, a poster of a panda on the door to the former pantry now a house for two heaters one for air and one for water and the vents ducts and pipes for each, old flowerpots, the hall to the door to the hall, full of boxes of Angel Hair books, the broken bassinet now a toybox with turtles and cups in it, a small space full of brown paper bags and cardboard six-pack wrappers, broom, dishes and pots, fruit on the hood of the stove, bottles and jars, teas and books, medicines foods and detergents, binoculars, the dishwasher, vinegar, garbage, Lewis' mother's old Scotch kooler, spices, another of George's plaid shirts, coats on hooks, a red tray; to the deadpan bathroom, a woman by Matisse in yellow and blue and an ordinary mercator projection of the world, potty chair, diaper pail for cloth diapers, plastic bag of used plastic diapers, toilet sink tub, bath toys an alligator that swims mechanically and a shark with teeth that is a mitt and a sponge, hideous old curling rug lying in the tub after yesterday's flood, hooks on the back of the door, layers of clothing hanging on them, a mirror, ointments and pills, razors poisons and soaps, shower curtains; to the main room the living room, two leaping goldfish, cornflower plant, jade tree, Wandering Jew not doing too well, another spider offshoot, purple weed I don't know the name of accidentally growing in a pot of sedum, Christmas tree fern with a sense of humor, whiskey, the main collapsing table covered with things, rocking chair, small wearing rug on the

33

golden wood floor, two couches with things on them, public school chairs with arms for principals at table, shelves of books and books in boxes, boxes of paper and stencils, two ring binders of photos since Worthington, my desk I steer and things, a standing lamp Nancy got us, a jacket by Joe and a blue shirt by George, a flower by Rosemary I don't remember the name of, a water color of a drapery by Rosemary done in Worthington, a drawing of Ted by Joe, a photo of Lewis by Gerard, pictures of the window out Main Street in different seasons, Main Street and Cliffwood Street, Our Lady of Perpetual Help-butterfly collage by Joe, a slinky male figure by Joe, a watch by George, some Kirschwasser, dead files and dead flies, magazines and library books, toys and balls, a stereo, four windows and the more frequent door.

An idea I have is to spend days walking nights writing never eating, sleep only when it rains and have an occasional beer.

Instead of dressing in a striped green suit you put a sheet between your legs and drape yourself upside down over the side of the bed becoming hysterical and then I know I can't rush you but when I see you can't sustain it I change the subject to something I know you want to know about and get the clothes on while you're still thinking but it only half works. Now two are done.

Below us the ardent hairdressers are beginning to welcome customers like spoiled children by pretending to be decadently faggy to please though they are not but they do please I guess they must their business thrives which one of the other mothers from nursery school said to me was what we all wanted after all though it seems cynical for me to say so it's the hairdressers who act like dogs from the Greek root *kynos*.

Next door the real gay men have already left for work in different local restaurants as waiters and chefs but one of them tired of his lover and recently moved out, then they put a wrought iron grille on

34

their apartment door which you can see through unless they choose to close the little hatch behind it from the Anglo-Saxon, *hagan*.

Downstairs the behaviorist child psychologist may be waiting for patients he'll give candy to if they'll agree to have half as many tantrums as without the candy and next to him the old-fashioned eagle-scout-type young man-woman bakes some kind of mail-order pies for a living with different roommates, you can smell the smell of the pies mixing with the chemistry-class rotten-egg smell from the hairdressers' permanent waves, it's a three-story turn-of-the-century red brick apartment house where rich men's coachmen used to live with their families in the thirties in a small egocentric town.

Your drawings look more like faces with three eyes now no mouths yet and occasionally an airplane or a low flower or the moon going from banana to carrot to orange every day and every month, red green and blue like t.v. or what you seem to be wearing.

Where's the chair it's in the pail put the person in it, is it the teacher's chair, I used to go to New York yesterday and have my hair shampooed, maybe it's a sparrow maybe not maybe it's just a bird maybe you could get me a big watch when Peggy comes look at that moon it's the middle of the night again no it's not.

What an associative way to live this is, dreams of hearts beating like sudden mountain peaks I can see in my chest like other breasts then in one vertiginous moment I can forget all but the reunion and your original face, two shirts each under overalls over tights under shoes then one sweater, outer suits with legs or leggings, mittens attached, hats and overshoes. Everybody wanting something or nothing to be done to them, then one of the shoes falls off again.

I have an image of a beautiful man or woman who walks in the door like Christ and earnestly spends some time with us like the UPS man does.

If only people would read more books but the world could still come to an end by colliding with bouncing babies banging spoons on cups that fly off the table, you can't pick up something you see on a page, it's too windy, you now speak something like Japanese, we found all the people last night and this morning they are spinning or poised.

I'm not playing. I'm cleaning though I'm crawling around. Are these dishes clean or dirty. I'm afraid not. Shit. The trees lose their leaves so you can see through them. A man and a dog in a yard. A person who doesn't have friends must explain himself to strangers. Sometimes your mother does on the phone, which religion is it that doesn't deny the lost self. Old morning prayers said in the cold church. Dear mother dear mother.

So for a second there's a chill in the season's gray air like warm structure and psychology, tickle tickle, I put the dozer, what do you call a person looking for water, on top of the Greyhound bus, dowser, and push to distract you from eating a person like I did. I'm glad I don't have only one eye. He's the kind of guy who shouldn't work in a window, I mean the printer.

I learn from the rigorous laughing of love to be more quiet in the morning especially if the dismal streets unearth a hideous memory of death, I've gotten so used to it I'm sorry I said that.

If we're all wrong about everything, the life so short and the craft so long to learn, the assay so hard, so sharp the conquering, the dreadful joy that passes so quick and then being left alone again, what I mean is love astonishes my feeling with its wonderful working so ardently so painfully that when I'm thinking about such certainty I don't know like the earth if I'm floating or sinking.

I don't know why we sleep or wake or why one dreams a fast bombastic image and the other memory's faintest trace which anyway haunts the day, if you look hard through the flawed window glass you can begin to see the lightest rain or snow but it's not there, now I can see it on the books and on the walls, it's in my eyes, I shouldn't even mention it, yet do you see it.

The paintings are finished so fast they are nice, what makes you know one is done. I can't see my eyes but I can see yours painted blue this year and I am in them. The leaping frog broke, it's broken.

Am I so modest as this time of day assumes I've learned, have I lost my tough or punk part among these kids who write on lines between the windows where I imitate them after they cover the walls with notes on making a face generous or a house a cave. Is all the mornings' cold-blooded conflict appointed to visions out the willful window, what are poetry's themes, grotesque little figures released by a spring from a box when the lid is lifted by another, I jump up to rescue an old reputation for immoral misfortune as one who does low dishonest work for another who suffers, my brother who pays me in sarcastic dogs for my writing, a swindle, I eat the leavings like the jackal after the lion is done, I know nothing practically like the wolf or a tasteless seed nonetheless edible, a perjured witness, straw man, an impostor, a jackstraw in a jumbled heap of pick-up sticks in a game, the peaceful steps from earth to heaven, monkey to exaltation, Jacob's ladder just a simple blue and white flower, my father, have I left anything out, why have I been forsaken for this joy.

Now we're almost ready, pity the race with the day if there's a reason to be sad or thinking ahead of everything so as we're leaving the house we must also be dying but you aren't, with my gloves on I gulp what you left in your cup just in case something small would be all the difference, still carrying you as a talisman, I'm dying to get to the post office.

· PART THREE ·

he dark brown stairs
Towards the doors
Of this house
          Wisdom's gray sky remembers
Snow is white crystals
Hall mirror,
Misaligned and broken strollers,
               Sex and going out
What there is of snow icing
The path plowed over the ground
Which is a story
        Earth's surface, lovers' intentions
Astounded as no one's around us
                A woman two children a man
Good morning or hello
It's not that cold
        The gray-brown mountains or hills
Are in a lifting cloud over Under Mountain Road
Often there's a cloud on the town, the town is on a mountain

Or halfway up a ridge declining north to south,
North is the Church on the Hill and the older cemetery
Here lies the town's first settler Jonathan Hinsdale
An innkeeper who had a daughter named Rhoda
South is the road to Stockbridge, north to Pittsfield
East is the rest of the village's houses toward another hill
West the route to Richmond, formerly Ephraim
There's no river and no river valley
It's an arbitrary place for a town
Just an inn on the road to fill up space
There are some brooks and ponds, Yokun, Marsh and Lily
East of Lenox Center the railroad runs along the Housatonic
Nearby there are the former homes
Of Edith Wharton, Nathaniel Hawthorne, Herman Melville,
William Cullen Bryant and Edith Wharton's mother-in-law,
The birthplace of W. E. B. DuBois,
And places Oliver Wendell Holmes frequented

                              Hawthorne said,
"I detest it! I hate Berkshire with all my whole soul
And would joyfully see its mountains laid flat . . .
One knows not for ten minutes
Whether he is too cold or too hot."

                    Lenox
Used to be called Yokuntown after Chief Yokun,
A Mahican of the River Tribe who lived by the Hudson
In good weather they hunted in the Berkshires,
Not fools enough to live here what they call year-round
Charles Lenox was the third Duke of Richmond,
Great grandson of King Charles II

                         Now the town's rich people
Live on Yokun Avenue near the private country club
And the invisible brook

                   Wisdom's wives and children
Surround the town like hills all alone like soldiers
It's quiet, there's the air

               In the important post office
We open Box 718 which is a drawer like the morgue,

People are either smiling or mad because of Xmas
There's another birthday card for Sophia from Julius and Julia,
A Penny Saver, a bank statement and a bill from Weleda,
No letters, checks or invitations change the world
Lewis closes the mail drawer and drops his glasses,
One of the lenses flies out, he throws up his hands
                                        And says
"What's the use?" Then Marie trips over her own boots
And hits her head on a brick
                        Sophia's mittens come off,
The disappearing scene from a dream I'd remember is lost
To comparisons of past exertion for the slight Main Street hill,
I blink at seeing, being seen a little
                                I wonder why we write at all
These trees have seen all this before
But they are glad of an encore
                        There's the gray sky
Above Lilac Park to the west where the weather comes from
Someone stole the lights from the town Xmas tree
                                        Often memory
Lends images to looking past the town close to the trees
Into the forest I saw while rehearsing for this narration,
It's a piece or a dream or a story or book, exciting invention,
We cross the street getting a line for a poem from right of way
But the neat dry bank is always the same big loss, even today
Though the pigeons from our roof feed in the yard next door
We are still as poor
                A little courtesy won't kill you, it says
On the Commonwealth of Massachusetts 1978 car inspection sticker,
Lock it, pocket the key
                        In winter you can see
In to the library yard from the street
                                Three Little Kittens
And There's a Wocket in My Pocket are overdue, we go in,
There's a sign on the door that from the first of the year
Library hours will be curtailed due to fuel prices
I feel the library should be colder and open longer hours

But I would rather see the downfall of the Shah
Everybody's autobiography is in this library
There's Noah's Ark, I go down the narrow Victorian hall
To find *Alone* and *Alive,* two ladies talk of Bible classes,
The man who tends the yard goes out by the locked gate,
The loud noon siren sounds from the town hall,
The library clock chimes twelve times
                                        We borrow
Pepys' *Diaries* and Drinkwater's book on Pepys,
Bit Between My Teeth by Edmund Wilson, *Alone,*
The Little Lamb and *Curious George*
                              Tantara!
It's a sound echoic of the trumpet's blast
Marie Maria Callas is having a tantrum in the library
She won't surrender her books, she won't put on her coat
It's a violent willful outburst of rage and annoyance
Like not having a room of one's own or the love of another
It's a fit of bad temper caused by the extremes of temperature
Nothing is mixed properly in her, she is excessive, rude,
Full of drama, intense fits of pitched proportion, freaking out,
She is hard and soft at once, hot and suddenly cool, mad,
She needs water, she neads kneading, she is not at all
Proportionate to the energy expended, how resilient is she?
Her frame of mind is readily angered and enraged,
She has a temper, it's a bad temper, she's really mad,
Her disposition is bad, her humor is excitable, volatile,
Her temperament is choleric hence she indulges excessively
In this fantastic outburst of kicking and resisting
In which the pitch of the tones of her loudest screams
Is like an electrically driven car to the consistent sun's
Hottest spots, she is fiery and dark, nothing tempers it,
It's her nature, she is bored, she's magnetic,
Her elbows won't bend into the sleeves of the dumb coat,
She has the strength of a thousand women and men, opposites,
The veins in her neck bulge with rage, rapid and combust,
She is exhausted, forced into the coat because of the cold,
She begs kisses in love's collaboration with some remorse,

44

The best thing is to take her away fast, make the change,
She looks a mess from her bout with what's intense and what's not,
She flies into a charming contrariness which totally belies
That for her down was up and water milk, breath unallowed
And language the false start to love it is, how unknown it is,
Leaping and flying into the cold, we breathe
                                        In winter we are nearer
The protecting mountains, in love we are obviously close
To rage, in another civilization a simple temper tantrum
Might not seem as threatening as an isolating storm
Still why not?
                    But why do we live here?
                                        Incorporated in 1767,
This town's not very old like hotdogs and Pampers
Everybody who visits us finds it kind of unwitting
To walk around a town like any other, just a place
Except it's New England which is defended, tight and cold
I'd rather live someplace higher, warmer and a little freer
Where money was like matches and words were wine
But as it is Lenox is okay for us as a family,
Two writers and two babies each of whom have each other
Still somehow beyond the community of local people
Some of whom are limited, bigoted, stodgy or mean
Others among them love nature and certain kinds of art
And a man we know who lives alone here says he's lonely
He just reads, drinks, keeps a journal and sniffs cocaine
The town adolescents shout and skid around in their cars
And leave half-empty bottles of Jack Daniels in the park
The high school imported a black man from Harlem to play on
Their championship basketball team, the Lenox Millionaires
And the rumor is the schools are so bad the students
Don't always learn to really read and write in sentences
Hockey's a big thing I don't know anything about it
Alot of cars have "Lenox Scholardollar Day" stickers
Which means they want to give money to the un-athletic kids
Zoning, sewers and taxes concern all the owners of private property
And the town is run tightly with an eye to tourists' money

But there's no other industry except for G. E.

                          Lewis' mother
Says we're snobs and we only think about poetry

                                It's true
There's something about America that's unthinkable
Like the style my mother thought she ought to be accustomed to
Because her mother had convinced her she was better than all this
Whatever this is, but not good enough to slough off the religion
Of the simple joys of poverty, humility and fear

                           And so
She gave my economic father the business religiously
And they both died young having said, if we didn't spend this money
To go on a vacation, we might have to spend it if we got sick
Without understanding that once bereft we've more to lose
And energy in the world mainly comes
From the hearts of the homeostatic people in it
Who hopscotch around, either picking up the stone or kicking it
And should be left alone without invasions or savings
Though there are masses and classes of people,

                         I don't deny it
What but the impulse to move and speak

                         Can change the world
Where should we move

                 Who is this person speaking
Who am I speaking to

               To you whom I love,

                    Can I say that?
I can't stand to watch the people leaving
Shear Design, that's the hairdressers' place, looking like
The Man from Atlantis or Farrah Fawcett Majors or like
Men who invidiously wish to be like

                   The unspeakable Shah of Iran
In their dealings with the world

                Now withdrawing, now attainable,
Rich with a drastic face for the hopelessly bitter people
Or the old story of the ludicrous young man in business
Flattering the aging woman with the greed of his attention

To further and simultaneously subvert the relentless image
Of the attitude of his mother to his father
                              Maybe here
My own moralism smacks of my neighbors' inherited tight-lipped looks,
These judgmental rugged individuals tense in the rigid morning
Like a memory of a funeral
                              Good day
                                    I'll defend your dismay
Parents, come to the hurricane
To protest the children learning in the usual way
To eat and adore
                    No that's not what I saw!
                                        Just beyond
The civilized town are places everyone goes by car,
Sears, Zayre's and King's, Stop 'n' Shop and the Price Chopper
Which is cheaper because they don't use union labor
Big mothers steer carts with kids past the things
And something called malls are the big thing now
With indoor gardens and no windows where whole families can go
Even on the weekends for pleasure and to buy things
But the malls seem to ruin the lives of the local people
And are all caught up in hideous deals with fraudulent corporations
From the outside these agglomerations look like artless spaceships
Buried into the ground surrounded by cars and some trees in space
And one of the problems with them is that such blatant flatness
Creates winds so fierce in winter one cannot walk
Inside are millions of the objects of novelty and fast-food to eat
In imitation of being rich like kings and being brought things,
Of being surfeited and entertained like queens vomiting
To be able to assimilate more which there isn't room for
In the spaceless closeted private-property house rendered valuable
Lately by the inability to see another house from it
Though in a state like this it's nice to be alone
                                        I'll trade you
We go on anyway
                    The hotel's deserted today
                                        Red berries,

47

This is the windiest corner of our walk, the most bitter,
The southern boundary of the circumscribed town, branches fallen
On each heart of every man and woman if they are they (invasion
Of the body snatchers) they seem to walk more tentatively
                                        As we do
Like a step on the ice of the wisdom of the temperamental sky
Like cars go fast because they mean everything headfirst
Like need and desire, money fame and all kinds of love
Now to creep without aggression or the protected passion
Of a real man or woman through this pile of beautiful ice
As if to slip away means nothing,
                        Has no word or expression
Like the baby's desire to swallow all the eggshells
Like nesting birds
                The strollers make a roar
                                Except for cars
We practically see only white or black or gray today
We look and we see
                Peripatetic
                        Like the police the police,
If it were noon the noon siren would just have frightened us,
Voting, the energetic town government, so clean and full of men
Who make sure the eyes of the people if nothing worse avoid
Flashing and neon signs and flagrant cheap posters and designs,
Street vendors and the uncut grass
                                Last summer
They even cut down the only blackberry bush in town
And the library had to lose its two dramatic elms
                                It's 12:15 p.m.
Everything circumscribed but what of nature's still around,
No place any different but for the limits of fear and love,
We love to walk for the rhythm of the heights to write
Going forward on foot by sights leaves the self alone at home
Something might happen or nothing, old lines, I might even die,
Ice and storms could crack the maples in their immobile ages,
Sentimental telephone cables are buried in the center of town
Not with a view to Mount Greylock

                                        You've done all this before
Nothing happens
                        Let's go over it again
                                        You've walked around
We're turning nearer home we meet the librarian who's got
An interesting hat, if it's not too cold or hot
We see the whole town every day, two square blocks
With alleys, shortcuts, the town clock and two weathercocks,
The Lemon Tree, Cimini's, the Crazy Horse, Lilac Park,
The first dentist, the dramatic post office, the Academy landmark,
Amoco Station, Dr. Tosk's, Loeb's Foodmart, Hagyard's Drugs,
Mole and Mole, the Lenox Library, Whitestone Photo, two icy fireplugs,
Two banks, Curtis Hotel, Town Hall, firehouse, police station,
Dee's Department Store, Four Seasons Travel-bus stop combination,
Different Drummer, Coffee Break, Candlelight Inn, Gateways Inn,
Community Center, Kelly's Irish Inn, Paddlewicker, Village Inn,
Nora's, Little Anthony's, David Herrick's, the pizza place,
The Arcadian Shop, Lucy Lou's, the second dentist, an empty space,
Spiritus Mundi, Clearwater, the greasy spoon, Michele the baker,
Buxton's Hardware, Elm Court Florists, the Bookstore, the shoemaker,
Heritage House, Just a Second, I've skipped the churches & Church Street
Between Housatonic and Franklin where the two package stores meet
The Golden Needle, Mainstream Woodworks, the former Yoghurt Rhapsody,
Glad Rags, The Restaurant, the laundromat and an art gallery,
I skipped Hawthorne Press which is off the main route
And the nursery school though we often go by foot
                                        In the animistic city
We saw the street was our hallway and in the country
The house the mind but this still village is an embarrassing relative
Below the flagpole's a dedication to all men and women in all wars
Under men's stern hats the suppression of all illuminating books
Behind their eyes the hideous secret of the emptiness of stuff
In the center of town an obelisk for the Revolutionary War
Under the counter Playboy, Trojans, Tahitis and contraceptive cream
On top of the two sisters' white brick house, a man on the roof
In the driveway near defunct Rapid Repair their bulldog defecating
In the greasy spoon the acting Chief of Police eating liver

On Main Street Mr. Mole gets into his Dodge Wagoneer

Nursing homes

And housing for the elderly surround the town
There's a one-story brick institutional place with a parking lot
In a small valley on Sunset Street next to William Shirer's house,
There's a home for women in an old house at the corner of Main
And Franklin Streets with a Japanese maple and tiger lilies in the yard,
There's an odd place near the nursery school named Turnure Terrace,
A low motel-like conglomeration of various connected versions
Of slightly different kinds of pseudo-Colonial architecture
With a kind of fire station and an American flag in the middle of it,
The residents of this place got mad when they saw nude kids wading
It seems alot of local people are more than a hundred years old
They always say the secret is they never smoked or drank
Two of these centenarians are driven in an old black convertible
As a part of all the town parades

Shell-shocked war veterans

Live in a home in a house at the top of the Lenox hill
They're alot like us, always muttering to invisible
Walkie-talkies and drinking beer and coffee in the doorways
Leering at the children in a greater attempt at love or seeing
Than the bourgeoisie's idiotic fascination with a tantrum
Sometimes everyone in the town seems to be a shell-shocked veteran
There's the man-who-smokes-Marlboros-down-into-the-ground
We haven't seen him for a while

Up the street there's the funeral home

Here's Nora's World of Fashion and the clumsy mannikin with one hand
In the vestibule, limitless childhood room without use between doors,
Leave your boots in the vestibule but don't get locked out,
Jump up and down before you come to the Formica kitchen table
Of your forsworn house, don't go to sleep if there's an ant in your ear
Otherwise you'll die, parked cars are like sleeping lions, watch out,
Safety from memory is in the pathless woods at night

One day

Is one dark day one day it's foggy one foggy day's ice storm
One fog's rehearsal one faster fog's threatening one better snow
Snow's rehearsal midwinter day one midwinter day's gray is better

Winter one better do me one better one faster one ice one day
One faster day one winning fast the snow is steaming ice cracks
Even to evening's unstable snow, moon past midnight
                                        One night
We went out for a minute in winter to see the fog together
And a deer or a bear made a noise like a horse next to us,
We ran away
                Once there was a banging at the door and a raccoon
Was hanging outside upside down
                                        Once when I was a girl
I answered the bell and Fred had put a lobster on the steps
And run away
                Once I had a dream I went to the door and there
Was an American Indian and a lion, I used to dream it all the time
And in the middle of the night in the room full of shadows
I used to tell my sister
                        "I'm not me, I'm someone else!"
And then I would creep out of bed over to scare her
                                        We took turns
Going down to the cellar alone in the dark
                                Hold my hand,
Let's cross the street, something about mothers all of them
I can't remember how I met her there's something inexorable about her
As if there were nothing completely new to offer or to render
As if whatever's new must be turned back and redone by force
Exactly the way we secretly know everything if you believe that
I do, I can hear the voice of another though I don't want to
In a voice I thought had been mine, now just rehearsing
To make the future the past in little steps like a baby leaps
To simulate walking at first and then forgets all about it
Only to remember to learn it faster later like she imitates
The movements of your lips not the sounds
                                        I swear I know it's only
The fantastic hedonistic narcissism
                                (Like the mother who said
The best thing is he looks just like me)
                                Of having another self

51

So half-combined with our lovers and us so stuck on our own
Mothers and fathers that makes us willing to endure our own wills
Again in children and love them, soft skin, the biological thing
Milked by the Catholics is that you'd die for them like a martyr
In the urgency of love's preservation like a rule
                                        The amazing thing
Is if they didn't take so long to grow up and live without us,
They'd never learn to love or even change
                                        Should I say all this?
I'm sure everybody knows it already
                                        Even though we live
Neither in a tribe nor a community nor near a grandfather
But in these rude, private and ignorant separate houses
Where love is like fame and fame is more like sin
And for love to be so tricky for a family is just asking for it,
Something about mothers
                        A list
                                I need to go to the health food store
To get a bottle of milk and a piece of Laughing Grasshopper tofu
You think something like a book will change the world, don't you?
I do, I take pleasure in taking the milk with the most cream
But I don't understand why we have to be repeaters like criminals
The bread at the bakery is lively, expensive and pretentiously thick
My mother's mother was a stocky stolid woman who rewarded us
With intense glances through her spectacles and miniscule tips,
My mother had a sharp intelligence denuded by religion and remorse,
Lewis' mother is tense, complex, worried and empathetically competitive,
Ed's mother was sharp and comforting, she was always praising you,
Peggy's mother is long-suffering, gracious in her Catholic survival,
Grace's mother is almost virulent in her heady raucous love,
Vito's mother is self-deprecating, kind and masochistic,
My first boyfriend's mother was jealous, suspicious and sexy,
Clark's mother is smart, praising and very short like his father,
Ted's and Alice's mothers sound adaptable to me
                                        Of all the people I know
I sometimes think of Peggy, Nancy, Lewis, Grace, Ted and David
As being my mother now but a mother is never another,

52

She is still you, almost by rote
                              There are certain dead writers
Who are like mothers who are more like moths
Coming to the light at night like friends
                              You and I
Each learned to love so well we even still love to steal
Though we hardly ever do since we met unless we have to
As if a theory of writing poetry is useful whereas the poem is not
Let's go in to the bookstore to see Matthew Tannenbaum
The dream figure of the boy-father-mother who turns into
The recalcitrant bookseller as we do
                              I look over the shoulder
Of a girl flipping through the pages of a book of women's faces
All beauties, bigger than life, black and white
                              Scavullo on Beauty
You study the poetry and read magazines upstairs
                              Let me tell you
The titles of all the current books:
                    The Suicide Cult, The Ends of Power,
The Origin of the Brunists, Invasion of the Body Snatchers,
War and Remembrance, The Winds of War, The Dogs of War, Dog Soldiers,
Mommie Dearest, My Moby Dick, My Mother Myself, By Myself, Uncle,
Mortal Friends, Nappy Edges, Tender Miracles,
Song of Solomon, Delta of Venus, The Women's Room,
Ladies Man, Six Men, The Water-Method Man, Watership Down,
The Night People, Shepherds of the Night, A Dream Journey,
Daniel Martin, Delmore Schwartz, Edith Wharton,
Time and Again, Better Times Than These, Centennial,
The Professor of Desire, The Honorable Schoolboy,
Heart Beat, The Third Mind, Jack's Book,
Beasts, The Magus, The Flounder, The Fabricator,
Words of Advice, Secrets and Surprises, Dispatches,
Prelude to Terror, Full Disclosure, Final Payments,
The World of Damon Runyon, The Stories of John Cheever,
Someone Is Killing the Great Chefs of Europe, Praxis,
The Annotated Shakespeare, The Last Best Hope
And *Chesapeake*

Now Marie says her boots are getting too hot
We run the few yards to the market in the deep and cheerful snow
To be insulted in our love by the profligacy of so much stuff
To market to market to buy a fat pig
Home again home again jiggety jig
There's the State Line Potato Chip truck
                                                We all go
In the door of the mausoleum store lit like a jailcell
To get spaghetti, oranges, juice, yellow peas and some cheese
Someone stops us to say Marie is growing like a weed again
And they can't believe how recently it seems Sophia was born
I can't get Marie in the cart too well with her Korean boots on
In the back with the butcher a woman judges a long slab of pork
Now I get to see it sawed in half under the buzzing fluorescents
Could you saw the bone she buxom says mister don't you have any bones
What are you a man or a woman today, I think I gave your husband
The wrong cheese yesterday, that's o.k., we live in a society where
Clean independence of the past seems best and the ability to eat
All that filthy meat is more prized than love and poetry's family
Which is hungry and impatient for munificent dreams and stories
Marie's had three oranges already, the checkout woman is surly,
She throws the peels away and packs my bag
                                                I write a check, $3.34
Lewis who was loitering near the lentils and peas with Sophia
Meets us at the doors, today our combined ages add up to 71 years
And all together we weigh 350 pounds, the temperature's 28 degrees,
It's 1:15 p.m.
                        We're going home with what we can have to carry,
Having had to pay for it
                                        And the sun comes out
And just on the path one last look at the mountains changing
Now they are crumbling like the wrong Roquefort cheese
And it's the end of the moon having piteously given its last quarter
To the dawn, world's end, beginning of niggardly winter, the nadir
Of some relation to the culminating sun, intensest of storms to come,
Sickening holidays, cold rooms and running out of money again,
Nothing to do but poetry, love letters and babies, hope for spring

Coming to please us because now we are parents, that love shoots
Mechanically from an automatic eye to the length of the line,
The distance to its subject centered in a field of cheerful snow
Past to the deep transparent trees, the sharp sensible horizon
Of the celestial sphere from which we will not drop off
                                                    And now
I've a wistful desire to stay outside
                              It's not really cold,
And roll with the babies in the snow till I get older
Maybe we could be outside almost all the time like sex and lists
Of music to hear to remember to laugh at whatever's forgotten
Doesn't have to be gone out again for
                                    Staying in
And sex is memory's intensity
                              The year's least day
Lost in the house of love's safe locks,
Movement's chance perfidy.

· PART FOUR ·

ome Clark's waiting for us. The last time
Celia was at our house she drew pictures of all of us and put whiskers
on Lewis and Clark, the whiskers looked like small pins sticking in
their chins.

Getting Marie to climb the stairs is like the time I tried to
drive to Nova Scotia in one stretch and the wheels kept flying off the
car and we'd stop every hundred miles or so to have them soldered
back on, it wasn't that the wheels flew off exactly but we kept getting
flat tires and when you took the wrench and tried to unscrew the
bolts the whole thing like a pin that kept the tire on would snap off.
By the time we might've been almost in time to make the ferry from
Portland we were so tired we had to lie down in the grass in some
rest stop under the horrible sun and later we got seasick and couldn't
sleep on the boat though we'd paid to get a cabin to rest in. In Halifax
they sell miniature meat sandwiches in the butcher shops. Marie says
her boots are too heavy for her to drag her feet up the stairs but if she
has something to carry like her sheet or a branch or a toy, you can

offer to carry it for her and then she'll walk up. Or like today one of us has to make two trips because of Sophia and the groceries.

Clark's brought us a bushel of apples, it's already on the table when we come in. Once Tolstoy leaped on his father-in-law's shoulder in a moment of joy. And Wagner once stood on his head during rehearsals, he became so excited. Beethoven felt that his father was not his real father and perhaps he was the son of some king or royal person.

We have to wear so much clothing it's as if we were in the Antarctic. Once one of the Antarctic explorers got frostbitten and the soles of his feet came off, he had to sew them back on; another's eyes turned from brown to blue. When they walked all day or all night trying to get to the Pole, all they would talk about was food because they were so hungry. They would vote on whose idea for something to eat sounded best. I think this was on one of Shackleton's or Scott's expeditions. One of the winning foods was roasted meat wrapped in bacon and baked in a pastry crust. It must've been Shackleton's because Frank Wild invented a sauce for it that became known as Wild Sauce, but I can't remember what was in it, maybe it was something sweet. They would dream about food all the time, they would dream the waiters couldn't hear them shout their orders or when the food came it was suddenly ashes.

Clark sits down but he can't stay long, he's on his way to pick up Susan and Celia to go to Providence for Christmas. Shackleton's men invented a game or a method of dividing up the food. They'd make equal portions but everybody was so hungry that one man would close his eyes and say who each cup of what they called hoosh would belong to so nobody would feel he was being even slightly cheated.

Marie is so impatient to get her heavy clothes off she reminds me of Lewis' parents who, when it's time to do something like pack up the car, create such an atmosphere of confusion where they each have a different idea of what to do next and its logistics that everybody in the family starts talking at once and then somebody inevitably gets mad and says, you do what you want but don't say I didn't warn you that you were doing it all wrong. My parents also used to think it was important to be what they called systematic in their packing and unpacking and Lewis remembers how his father used to have to struggle to finally get the trunk of the car closed on all the stuff. My father once slammed the trunk closed on his own hand, then at least my mother got to do the driving without there having to be a big discussion about that. My father used to keep an exact record of all the mileage traveled and how much gas it took so he could figure out later how many miles per gallon he was getting and at what cost. And all in such a beautiful hand with a good pen the notebooks were wonderful to look at and appeared precious. When I was moving out of my first apartment, Ted and Ed vied to see who could pack the truck full of stuff better and faster, then we all went to have some drinks at the Orchidia and Ted had a Grasshopper.

The sun is shining really brightly now. Yesterday Brys, Claire's husband, drove me down to nursery school with Jonas and Marie because Claire went to New York to take care of her mother. When we got to the dirt road that goes to the school the truck swerved off a little and got stuck in the ice. The road was so icy when we tried to walk none of us could stand up. Then Cara and her father told us there wasn't any school anyway.

Now's the best time to be a mother, everybody's hungry when we first get home, Marie wants another orange, she asked for it three times before she got her coat off, Sophia needs lunch before her nap, Lewis coffee bread and butter, Clark and I want beers but I guess it's too early so we just share one. David once told me it was probably dangerous to drink more than eleven cups of coffee a day. When I first went to see him I drank alot of coffee because I had to get up early to meet my appointments which he thought was healthy for me, though it wasn't very early. The first time we kissed he said, you have sweet breath, and then once later we began to make love and he said, you like it.

Clark hasn't taken off his coat and now he has to go. The bushel of apples has candy canes too and some honey and cheese. Anne Bradstreet had eight children, she lived in Boston around 1650 and the manuscript of her first book of poems was taken to England and published without her knowing anything about it. Her father was the governor of Massachusetts and after she died her husband was too.

Lewis goes into his room to work. Someone said Harriet Beecher Stowe became quite crazy towards the end of her life and pretended she was selling matches on the street. Margaret Fuller was an egomaniac and said at one point she had at last decided she accepted the universe. Then Carlyle evidently said it was a good thing she did.

Now there's so much to do for a while, alot of little things, getting the dumb objects out of the bag, peeling oranges, making some space to slice bread, washing the tray and to find a clean cup and to have to deal with the awful sink. I don't even look up, there is a window in the kitchen. Rudy Burckhardt says alot of his photographs are all looking down at an angle, maybe influenced by Yvonne who paints views looking down from way up in an airplane. He says his look down from about 5 feet 9 inches.

It's so automatic at this time of day to do some of the same things I feel like a machine. Ed loved emergencies, he said he wanted to be a machine, I wonder if he still does. One time Barry's girlfriend Britta who lived upstairs fainted dead away and Ed resuscitated her. But before he did he told me to get somebody on the phone, but I couldn't find the phone and panicked and I didn't find out till much later that Barry and Britta didn't have a phone because they were always completely broke.

Marie asks me what do turtles eat, then squirrels, rabbits and lions. I tell her lions eat meat. Dr. Incao who's an anthroposophist which means he adheres to the philosophy of Rudolf Steiner, said children shouldn't have any meat until they're three years old, it makes them too brittle. He says people are either hard or soft and when he examines you he gently feels your forearm and fingers. Lewis' niece Joanna was eating liver from a jar when she was two months old. Margaret Mead says everybody's different ways of taking care of babies is a symptom of the American custom of never doing anything your mother or father did which has something to do with the pioneers, it's a sign of separation. Giraffes are vegetarians and they chew the cud like cows.

Sophia eats lunch playfully, she reminds me of a penguin or a porpoise or a whale or Buddha. A couple of weeks ago a bird got caught in the closet that has our air and water heaters in it. Then when we looked again so we could throw a pillow case over it and pick it up and release it as we once had to do with a pigeon who walked into Lewis' room through the open window, it was gone, I don't know how it got out. At Clark's house in the summer birds came in so frequently because there wasn't a screen door, I made a net like a butterfly net with a stick and a bag onions came in and then I would catch the bird and slide a piece of cardboard underneath the net and take the bird outside. Clark's house has such big windows sometimes the birds fly at them and dash themselves hard against the glass. Sometimes they are only stunned but once in a while they get hurt. I stayed there a couple of times while Clark and Susan were in California.

Marie pretends she's diving and swimming in a sea or pool of newspapers she's thrown around. She jumps from boxes of Ted's books in the kitchen. Once I was carried out by the current of the ocean at Rockaway and had to be rescued by a lifeguard. Though I was still afloat and hadn't had a chance to try to swim back to shore, one of the girls I was with panicked and began to go under. The lifeguard swam with one arm and pulled me back.

I chop onions for the sauce. St. Augustine hated the Greek language. My sister was supposed to be a Greek scholar and get a doctorate in Classics from Harvard, she had a Woodrow Wilson Fellowship but instead she decided she wanted to paint. I learned Greek from a nun at New Rochelle who taught us to sing the language in tones like Swedish. Once in Greek class one of the other students told me I had always reminded her of Antigone. She said this the day John Kennedy was murdered. It was a Friday and I had a ride to New York after class from a guy from Astoria who went to Iona and eventually became a policeman. When Marie talks now it sounds tonal like Swedish, it used to sound unaccented like French.

Marie's painting with tempera colors. Raphael once told me he thought Diane di Prima's work was difficult and somewhat crazy until he read mine, though he's sympathetic and sees our writing as a symptom of what he thinks of as the crazy times. William Shirer surely wouldn't like my work, he says Gertude Stein was a megalomaniac and the ugliest woman he ever saw and that her writing is just silly. I wonder what he'd have thought of Margaret Fuller Ossoli. Barry told Clark I shouldn't write about Lenox and he didn't like Lenox. Someone else said I was no longer a true experimentalist. Alex once said my writing was rude and Les thought my photographs in Memory were too pretty. Marie's paintings are bright and done quickly.

She is trying to execute a face. Susan said that after her father died her mother seemed to change and to become more relaxed. I remember my sister and me trying to encourage my mother to remarry and she would always say, who would want me? Then later she would say, don't ever marry, Bernadette, join the convent. But she meant because it's easier I think.

I see feathers floating down from the pigeons on the roof. When Sophia was born it was six in the morning and the pigeons were cooing like roosters. The midwife Betty said Philip meaning the doctor would like that sound but he hadn't come yet because he'd gotten caught in a blizzard without his snow tires and he had to drive really slowly. Also after a long labor Sophia began to come really suddenly but from what the midwife had told the doctor previously, he thought he had more time. He got here right after Sophia was born. But all the time she was about to be born, in between contractions the midwife would run to the window to look for his car, then I would call her back.

It's time for Sophia's nap, she needs to have her diaper changed first. My cousin Florence had two children in a flimsy small new house in Central Islip, Long Island. Her husband Nick who always wore black spent all his money at the racetrack. Once two of my uncles followed him there and saw he was with another woman. Though Nick and Florence could not get divorced because Florence was a Catholic, they began to live apart. Everybody in the family said he was a bad apple. Up till then the people who were whispered about were Uncle Charlie my father's brother who never married his wife Grace who was an alcoholic and bore the only son who had the Mayer name, and Uncle Ken who was a Lutheran and who induced his wife to practice birth control. In Lewis' family there are two cousins who fell in love and live together, Jerry and Bonnie. Jerry had a wife and two children before and his mother, Fanny, doesn't approve of Bonnie but Uncle Sammy, Bonnie's father, says he thinks it's o.k. But then Lewis' mother who is Fanny and Sammy's sister says what else could he say, he must make the best of it.

Sophia goes to sleep, she's attached to her pink blanket. Once Yuki called me up and invited me to go ice skating. He didn't know Lewis and I had just begun to live together. I haven't ice skated since

65

a retreat I went on in high school, we skated on a pond in the woods at night. It was a silent retreat but when the nuns went to bed all the girls would get together and sing "Chantilly Lace."

Marie says she wants to read a book before I fix the rest of the dinner. Verlaine had a terrible life, he was poor, a kind of vagabond, his wife forbade him to see his son, he had an affair with Rimbaud and he died of many different diseases. For years he was so sick he used to spend the winters in the hospital. He was famous and his son edited his works. Lewis was just reading a biography of him.

We read *Betsy and the Doctor* where Betsy falls out of a tree while she's at nursery school and hits her head on a stone. She goes to the doctor and not only does she have to have stitches but an injection in her head as well. Once an old friend of mine was driving me to the airport and she crashed into a taxi at Broadway and Houston Street. My head hit the windshield and when the police came they told me I should say I'm a model and sue. They called an ambulance but at the hospital they only ripped the cut apart in a rough way and rubbed it with something, then later a doctor had to remove the glass from my head after the cut was healed and it was only the day after the accident I realized it was my knee that was fractured. And my friend Kathy told me, "Maybe I did it on purpose." She said she was mad at me because she thought I might have slept with her boyfriend who was my sister's ex-husband. You can't even see the scar.

I love chopping vegetables where you do something to make something that is one idiosyncratic thing into many things all looking the same or identical, much like the vegetables' original seeds. How rapt attention is to doing this as if it were a story. I remember Bill saying how he and Beverly when they began to be short of money couldn't understand why when Clark wanted to buy Susan a Cuisinart, she said she didn't want one.

Everything is edible. It's a long story, coins or cubes or tree rings of carrots like the slices of trees that are tables in the library yard, canoes of celery like the clergy or something with strings attached, miniature trees of broccoli and if you are poor enough to want to cook the whole plant, their inevitable tree stumps that look like primitive clouds, Moses used to have cauliflower ears, now covered by curls like grated carrots, last-quarter moons of onions or bloated apostrophes, crumpled papers with typographical errors of chopped spinach or greens, unseaworthy boats of rigid turnips in which the survivors resort to cannibalism rather than eat the odoriferous boats, railroad ties for french fries, sleepers, the third estate, the common people, Oldenburgs to go into stew or a peasantish flying saucer for a meatloaf or the flapping wings of the memory of rich pounded veal where I am crushing flesh between waxed paper with a hammer in the kitchen if I can afford it, the commas of the cheapest small onions for the sauce, the olive oil's drops on the map of the pot of tomatoes, letters of the straight pasta and the Poons in the soup with Twomblys, arbitrary split moons of the half peas, the camera lenses of the lentils, homogenized script of the mass rice, foreplay with the nice knife at butter, my mother used to have a pressure cooker but she made it clear she was afraid it would explode any minute. When she cooked carrots in it she had a habit of saying, "It's too bad, they taste earthy."

We're only having spaghetti. Once on my mother's birthday which was April 4th, we went for a picnic to Clarence Fahnstock State Park and I refused to get out of the car. She also had a habit of regretting she hadn't married somebody rich, like "the man who used to take me out in a taxi."

Bright sun is on everything, it's on the ice on the roofs, on the wet street, on Marie in the kitchen, it's making parallelograms on the walls of the rooms. I like to play poker. Poe was an incessant gambler and Hawthorne got in trouble for gambling at school. Once I made a bluff so large I blushed, but I got away with it and won forty dollars.

Marie's spilled her milk again, no use crying over spilled milk. Wittgenstein says there is no such thing as a private language. I think it would be worth trying to make one. Sol Kripke solved the liar's paradox but I cannot understand his solution. Wittgenstein's house was furnished with old crates though he was not poor and when he came to eat at your house he would wash all the clean dishes over again himself before the meal because he was afraid they were not really clean. Once Lewis had a job teaching a rich woman to write and when I came home I saw a filthy glass filled with water on the table. He said he had given it to her to drink.

I think I'll have a beer. As a child Lewis had something wrong with his eyes which they now call amblyopia. Both his eyes didn't function at once and you have to wear a patch over the good eye to exercise the bad eye. Lewis thinks someday maybe he'll be blind and our daughters and I will have to read aloud to him all his abstruse books on Jewish mysticism just like Milton. He hasn't even read the New Testament yet but recently he asked me where Christ was born.

There's that cloud again muttering in the organized blue sky of love about diffidence. Sometimes as a child when I was out visiting relatives and I was bored and wanted to go home, I would throw up. It wasn't hard to do because my aunt made chocolate cake with orange flavoring and iced tea with orange juice in it and jello with slices of orange. My sister used to get bloody noses.

I call nursery school to find out when they'll be closed for Christmas and talk to Barbara about Chanukah. Margaret Fuller married an Italian revolutionary named Count Ossoli and had a child when she was thirty-seven. When they boarded the ship to come to New York, Margaret was so filled with foreboding she could not walk. The ship sank off the coast of Fire Island and she and her family were killed. Frank O'Hara was killed in an accident on Fire Island when he was also forty years old.

I clean the cutting board with a cloth and remember something so awful I can't relate it, now two things, not to ever tell them but just to say they have to do with jealousy. I can say stories are always remembered, after all they're not just made up like a dream. They're like dreams made to conform to the structure of remembering what is not a dream. I used to live with my first boyfriend in an unused kitchen in his family's house in Long Island City. They were a big Italian family, Bob's grandmother lived with them and they'd converted the basement into a big kitchen where we ate important meals and listened to the grandmother's stories of how her husband, when he first came to America, shot a man who made a pass at her or knifed him and had to go to jail. He had been a streetcleaner and she had a bad back and slept on a bed that was a board and had to wear a complicated corset. After my uncle died Bob's family wound up taking care of me, always trying to feed me steaks and keep me warm and to as they put it keep my mind off things so I took summer courses in psychology at Hunter. A Bolognese doctor they had sent me to said there was nothing wrong with me a good slap wouldn't cure. And the day I got out of the hospital in Queens where I had seen a woman die, I saw a man hit by a car and thrown a hundred feet in the air. Bob had an uncle who had an ulcer and always drank milk and secretly smoked. And another uncle who was a tool and die worker who died of something everyone in the family said was caused by his having eaten in too many Puerto Rican joints. Bob's sister nursed her babies discreetly with a diaper over her shoulder to cover her breast and her husband had a compost heap and grew the best vegetables, he was a carpenter named Bucky Presti. Bob's sister's best friend Carolyn was killed in a car accident. We slept in the kitchen practicing onanism but every time I began to seem crazy enough to collapse again they would assume I was just pregnant.

I make a note of what we'll need to eat for the next three days since the stores will be closed for Christmas. All this time I was living with Bob and his family I was trying to live with my grandfather in Ridgewood but the house only reminded me of death and my grandfather insisted that all the lights be out after nine o'clock. He'd come into my room and shout angrily but he never could remember who I was and he would call me Marie. When I went out at night he would double-lock the doors so I couldn't get back in.

The sauce is done. Then I went to visit a girlfriend of mine who was going to a Jesuit college in Syracuse. When I came home Bob met me at the airport, it was the first time I'd flown and I had fallen in love with someone and that was Ed. We went back to my house in Ridgewood, this was when I was trying to go to Barnard but it took me two hours to get there. Bob's mother had given me a wedding shower because my grandfather had given me my mother's diamond ring and she took that to mean we were engaged since she was worried anyway I'd get pregnant before we got married, though she was relieved that Bob wasn't queer after all. I didn't know anything about birth control. We had set a date for the wedding and arranged a reception but the place we were going to have it in burned down. Bob's mother worked as a maker of wedding gowns. So that night in my house I told Bob to watch me sleep because I was afraid to sleep otherwise. In the middle of the night I sat up in bed, he said, and asked him a question. After that he always understood that I was no longer in love with him. I didn't know what Ed wanted to do but a couple of days later he came to my house and said I want to live with you, meet me in two weeks. The night before I was supposed to leave I went out with Grace who a while before had been in such a bad car accident she was still walking with a cane. We went to a bar and I left with a minor league baseball player who had an MG, Grace left with somebody else and we met later at my house. I missed the taxi I had called to make the early plane but I caught a later one and when Grace woke up in my house all alone my grandfather mistook her for me even though she has red hair and he called her Bernie. When Grace left my neighbor Tex told her he'd seen the taxi and wondered what was going on, he's the one who had said when my father died, "Who's that?"

Now the dinner's ready, Marie says I want to say foody to Daddy. When Edmund was about four months old and Anselm must've been two, I visited Ted and Alice in Chicago and it was Ted's fortieth birthday. He made us cry and Edmund was crying too and Anselm was locked in his room in the morning because otherwise he wouldn't stay in bed just like Marie.

Marie and I talk about the weather while we eat together, Sophia's still asleep and Lewis is eating in his room. When the sun is out there are reflections on the ceiling of Marie's juice in a cup or my beer in a glass. A million times I remember seeing something moving in the peripheries of my vision just like this and wondering what is that. And being awed to find out it's really something instead of just nothing. Once I remember walking the length of a loft I lived in in a state of nervousness and seeing something which did turn out to be a mouse and then seeing something else which was my own reflection in the gray t.v. screen. As a child it was always interesting to go home tired in the back seat of a car at night. The shadows and the wash of other cars which are still waves even when I hear them now. But the best remembered perfection was the well-being of the feeling of lying awake through the night some hot night as a child thinking that the heat ought to keep limbs from touching and then floating from memory like a person on the sea.

This food is all eaten too fast, there were the designs of kitchen linoleum then in yellow and green and even in the bathroom, wallpaper covered with hazardous designs, a meticulous florid space to contemplate how one's finger might run over the pattern in a systematic way, to put it to memory so later when the beds have to be made and you want to make a point of not doing as you're told, it's Saturday morning, you can run that pattern automatically with a finger on your stunned thigh.

I ask are you finished, you seem to want mine. There's only time left to tell how the floors met the walls and we saw centipedes all the time crawling across the carpets which were green beneath the blue glass table which was a mirror with a plate of balls on it under the windows which on some days we cleaned but not too well so we wouldn't fall out like my mother did not but someone else's mother did and she died but my sister fell out once with a piece of cheese in her hand but she was so embarrassed and ashamed she didn't tell anyone and just got up after I had already tried to compare with her how sex for us might be different but then we got into trouble again and resorted to the cellar to tear each other's hair out and teach tongue-kissing.

Marie says let's read a book or something. Once I dreamed I answered the door and it was Ted and Charles Olson who was black, Charles was black, Ted was Ted Berrigan. The hall was covered with broken glass from Olson's having bumped his head on the transom. We all went to see Bill Berkson, we took him with us to wait for the Robert Browning bus which had brown and white checks on it. It didn't stop so we walked to Bloomingdale's, I was pushing a carriage. Ted became a part of the carriage and I couldn't get it over the curb because he was a person and had no wheels. The whole thing turns over but he doesn't get hurt. I buy a pair of earrings that are so heavy they make me dizzy. I steal ten dollars.

We read *Beady Bear*. It's a story of a toy panda bear who decides he ought to live in a cave but he can't fall asleep there because it's cold and he's nervous and then he just falls down and can't move because he needs to be wound up again by the child to whom he belongs, a boy named Thayer. I've had dreams that Rosemary becomes the editor of the New York Times and has a son, that I am a Marine and Bill Berkson is the head of my reserve unit, that Godard dies and comes back to life to make a movie, that Henry Miller shoots George Wallace, that Grace is in the Electoral College, that Picasso lives on Saturn, that Hawthorne turns into a white chicken, that Peggy has an aunt named l'Immortellement Mort Martine, that Ron trusted me, that I show John Cage the map for world improvement on my scarf, that Lewis Warsh falls on the railroad tracks in 1969.

I tell Marie a dream I had, I was floating down a river drinking Heinekens when I saw Grandma who was patting John on the back. Then Lewis and Peggy had to go somewhere together and I had to go and give a poetry reading but somebody told me it would take three hours to get there which meant I would miss my dinner. But I didn't care because I don't like to eat alone anyway. I stopped some cars on the West Side Highway to try and get a ride but the drivers were all mad and then I realized it was California where Moses lives I had to get to which would take three hours by plane, not by car. Then Patti Smith came in and turned off the t.v. Someone made some remarks about women and art. I didn't tell Marie the rest of the story which goes: when I got to the plane I was told I had to be the pilot but I kept postponing boarding because I didn't want anybody to tell me what to do, then the stewardess wouldn't let me into the cockpit of the jet because she said, someone who looks like you could never be supposed to be the pilot of a plane. Then the whole cockpit with all the co-pilots in it started crashing through the nose of the plane. Somebody seemed to catch it by the hair and Marie got scared and started running towards me crying mommy.

We read *The Tiny Tawny Kitten* next, it's the story of a cat who is afraid of everything, it's a female cat, she watches all the kinds of cats out at night from her window, the lean lanky alley cat, the spotted meat market cat, the gray ratcatcher cat and the striped firehouse cat. And the tiny tawny kitten was afraid, it says. Then what happens to her is once she unconsciously lashes out with her claws at an old loud dog and hisses at him and she becomes brave after that and even sleeps with him. Once I had a dream I was fighting in Vietnam, we were men and women. Other women kissed our hands, we were not called women. Our guns were filled with putty for ammunition, often they wouldn't fire. The battles were planned, we would fight for a few minutes then rest for a few hours. Most of the enemy shot themselves and not us. We were on a houseboat, there were many poets as guests.

Big Dog, Little Dog. Two dogs named Ted and Fred do every-thing the opposite of each other. They go to the mountains and get rooms in a small hotel. The big dog gets a bed that's too small and the little dog one that's too big. Neither of them can sleep. The next day a bird suggests to them they trade rooms. Both dogs go back to sleep for the rest of the day. That is all there is of that story. John Wayne wrote a letter to Barbara Walters saying Patty Hearst is being discriminated against because she is rich. He says if the nine hundred people in Guyana can be brainwashed to commit mass suicide then surely one pretty little girl could be coerced to rob a branch bank.

The Three Little Pigs. Three pigs who have hair on their chins are too poor to continue to live with their mother, they must support themselves. Two of them get eaten by the wolf because they build their houses out of flimsy materials. The third pig who has a brick house which he got by posing as a cripple, winds up boiling the wolf alive and eating him. Admiral Byrd was the first person to spend the winter alone at the South Pole. For a while he did well and wrote alot of speculations on the nature of the universe, then the stove in his hut began to poison him with fumes. He would collapse all the time and he had to force himself to eat, he kept the heat on only enough to survive and as the winter got colder, ice began to cover the walls, ceilings and even the floor. He told his men nothing was wrong but his messages in code reached them as indecipherable gibberish half the time, so they made a trip in the dark to rescue him.

Marie's asleep. Sekhmet the wife of Ptah said, "When I slay men my heart rejoices." Depicted with the head of a lioness, she was so brutal and unrelenting that to save the human race from extermi-nation Ra spread across the bloody battlefield seven thousand jugs of a magic potion made of beer and pomegranate juice. Sekhmet who was thirsty mistook it for human blood and became too drunk to continue slaughtering men. The human race was saved but to ap-pease Sekhmet, Ra decreed that on the twelfth day of the first month of winter, there should be brewed in her honor as many jugs of the phil-

74

ter as there were priestesses of the sun. "Hostile hostile is the 12th," says the calendar of lucky and unlucky days, "avoid seeing a mouse on this day, for it is the day when Ra gave the order to Sekhmet."

Popped-out-of-the-Fire: A girl lived there (with her brother and grandfather). Though the girl slept alone every night some person came to sleep with her. The person who came to sleep with her never spoke. He came to her there a long time. And then the girl became pregnant. She did not say anything of it, she was afraid to. Now this is what she thought. "I will paint my hand. That is the way I will find out who it may be." Indeed that is what she did. And then (in the night) she hugged him, she put her hand on his back. Now the people (men) were going to come out of the sweat house where they were sleeping. And so she watched in secret, and then all those people (men) came out. Indeed now she learned it was her own older brother who was sleeping with her. Then the girl became sick (from shame and grief she no longer ate, and then she died), and he also died, he starved himself (in his shame and grief), and that is why he died too. When she died her father laid her upon the fire. And he held an Indian blanket and the old man spoke thus, "Pop out on to this here!" Sure enough the baby popped out (from her scorching corpse). Now its grandfather brought it up.

Septimius Felton was a character of Hawthorne's who tried to create the elixir of life from some old Indian recipes of his aunt's and the secret information given to him by a soldier he shot during the Revolutionary War. On the soldier's grave a red flower grew, it was supposed to have been the last ingredient, sanguinaria sanguinaris, bloodroot, growing from the heart of a young man violently killed. But the flower was a hoax planted by the Englishman's lover who seduced Septimius and helped him make the potion which was now a deadly poison, then she drank it, confessed all and died. Then Hawthorne intimates that Septimius who loved knowledge too much inherited the English soldier's estate and became a boring landowner whose descendants had dull and lifeless eyes.

Joshua the son of Nun sent men to Jericho to spy for him. They went to the house of a harlot named Rahab. She hid them from the king because she said she knew the Lord had given them the land and had dried up the water of the Red Sea for them. In exchange for her help they agreed to spare her and her family from annihilation if she would hang a scarlet thread from her window.

I steal from the bed not to waken Marie. She's happy to sleep but will wake up angry. Sophia will wake up feeling good unless she's cold. In the morning if the sun shines which now it hardly ever does, Sophia gestures with grace towards the eastern window in her room. I set fire to the end of a cigarette and look out the kitchen window at the mess of ice on the trees, streets and roofs. No geese flying south, it's the awful solstice. This morning the axis of the earth began what the papers called its slow tilting return, the sun will last one minute longer and the nights will be shorter. Lately when the sun sets it breaks through the hat of cloud on the sky like a person on the street who only glances at you, and then it begins to snow. The sun catches your eye.

A calm sentence like a story. I used to know a man who had a dog and I followed their steps in the snow, I got into the habit of walking just as far as they did every day. At the same time I also knew a woman whose husband had seven guns. I used to know a woman who's the woman who married Neil Simon. I like the woman who used to work in the Lenox market, she never wears boots, then she retired. In New England the women are often more exciting than the men, Lewis thinks so too, I don't know why. There's a tribe somewhere where people say about the men, look how he's changed since he's had children, he looks awful!

Then soldiers came to relinquish and not fortify the wall and a meal was made of fish from the brazen sea and wine in vessels of brass and of every day that remained its work required that the day

76

be a woman and that the woman be pretending to be another woman, that anger is the father and anger is the child, death is food to remember history to tell, a big fat man with a white beard in a red suit who eats what we eat and is never cold even though he flies around the world in only air, dear mother, the church is still cold.

The language into which we put the order of stories from this kind of memory is a mesmerization of sins like the ones I made up which were my first stories because when I still had reason to confess I was free of even the venality of my tales, though told with love, and I could imagine coming up with enough lack of perfection to commit them or even obsessively put them in writing like a letter to a judge when I'm in prison, rather than just to speak them to one man who was a story in himself of a kind of outfit of supposed love which could turn to emnity or even lechery out of love, another love, in a minute, a story of the moment of the mystical body and cannibalistic frenzy laced with fierce and beautiful singing of songs in loud strong weak guilty and innocent voices below the organ tagging along behind the desire for a fantastic transforming love of what is beauty or ritual's idolatry of mystery among our historical family, all present in the church, though late, to tell us what to do next and how to have the pride to proceed.

Not the pride of devils who are fallen angels but the pride of angels who are faithful who subsume all love of other and the hideousness of possession under the vaulted ceiling which is standing for the life where the mind is like a sky over the earth and men and women are the homeostatic expressions of a universe given for a while to their multitudinous ideals of fateful love, land as homes and the principals of families and food, and the righteousness that activates the strongest of what's left of the men and women after wars are finished to excite the rest to some belief in gratuitous love and the inevitability of the sublime because life for almost everyone has its moments and but for that the whole thing is somewhat dead already, this was my great confusion.

The history of every historical thing including God but not including all men and women individually, is a violent mess like this ice. But for the spaces even hunchbacked history has allowed in between the famous and loud for something that's defined as what does please us. Which is perhaps this story of an intimate family, though you won't believe or will be unable to love it, driven to research love's limits in its present solitude as if each man or woman in the world was only one person with everything I've mentioned separate in him or she didn't represent any history at all though he or she had stories to tell and was just sitting kind of crazily before an open window in midwinter or thinking of the celebrating supper or sleeping on the independent bed or in the enclosed crib which in history could only be relentlessly plundered, in story a sensational death perhaps.

I am like a woman who says I am another woman, or a man who says I am another man. They sleep to rest, beginning to know another, like a story. Then we rest to recover something already gotten from what might be called its mother and father. Next our genius will amaze us like the rest we've had to discover of all we might ever be able to know. But not before, as the story now goes, the ones who discover it will be mythically lost having suffered wanting to unearth more than there is from what history's supposed to be, less than a baby, or the terrible criminal repeating memory which slows us down like a race a swift attack, a current of water in a river or the ocean's more famous undertow, this window of mine too badly designed to let air in yet too large to make sense, I only feel cold and I'm still here before it, young enough but still a mother, old enough to end the story that might have ended before me.

I have a sensation of waiting, you should call and tell me how the rest might go. Like an important letter, a whole different matter, if I only knew what I need to know. You call and I say in some way I already know all about it, I expected it. That's a story that might happen today, I don't dare to end as death is still bewildering, love might be a trick and you are another. But to be beginning I'll only say that to have you as love is like the history of this idiosyncrasy. If

78

that is not a story then I who have so far listened so much and now am beginning to be able to say something, which is another story, am surprised.

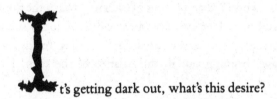t's getting dark out, what's this desire?

Sophia's awake, she slept late, she's not calm, she sounds hungry. Marie having slept lightly awakens. She cries, Sophia points to a banana. Marie's thirsty.

The sun begins to set, for a moment the room is pink, soon the snow will be blue. Branches thin out before the bright light, light glances off the tops of cars parked on ice like glass. Snow describes a pattern on a series of roofs, there's no one around.

Lewis comes in. Marie says we've gotta have Talking Heads dance music.

Close to the lower sun, more pink and more red, no clouds, isolation. Something red, a barn, the brightest part of the picture. Red brake lights Marie says are stars on the moving cars. The wet street is red.

Lewis dances with Marie. Sophia's caught by the light that's left, gold eyes wide brown almonds. Half her face is in darkness, her mouth is partly open. She's about to move her hand toward me, she stops, there's a blank sweetness in her interest. Marie stands behind her in the darkening light, her bright shirt. She grins, Sophia moves forward as if to leap or spring. Marie stiffens and pulls in her lips, it's a pose. Everything is red even daydreaming, biology, wildlife, Freud.

Sophia says yes, Marie gestures wildly with her arms in the air and pushes her chest out, she has Snoopy on her shirt. She says no.

Marie dances, red and blue. She's thoughtful, it's a running dance, stepping like an Indian the toes of each foot touch the floor before the sole and heel. Her eyes are open wide, she looks suddenly older. It's an arrogant dance, she turns, her hair flies, hands clasped together, elbows bending out in the balance of the turn, I catch her eye.

We eat supper, it's rye bread and cheese, Marie says I want to cut paper, she grabs a candy cane from the bushel of apples, Sophia grabs her cup and handles it well. Marie sees herself in the darkened window, she smiles, she's lost the candy.

We have a beer, we talk about a book and a grant. Sophia scratches at the wax on the cheese, Lewis makes faces. She eats small pieces of the soft cheese with her fingers.

Marie says children have candy my name is Betsy you'll get sticky. She calls Sophia baby brother, it's from a book. She says here's a mountain I made I cut it sharp and thick. Sophia plays with the butter, Marie says Jessica said nar for star and I'm afraid of the light.

Sophia sits on my lap playing with markers. She pulls them from a jar, opens them and puts them back. She does it repeatedly, Marie falls down.

Marie builds a farm from blocks, she puts two cows in a stall. Sophia takes them. Marie says don't destroy my farm. Sophia walks. They shout.

Marie wants Lewis to read *Curious George,* he doesn't want to. She says try it. What should we do with the bushel of apples?

Lewis says I'm not a pillow, then Marie does. They read *The Little Lamb.* He says to her there's a worm in your shirt I'll get it out. She says now say a snail.

Sophia tries to draw, she looks like a cat sitting upright, feet straight out wide apart, arm extended to drop a marker in the jar Marie begins to pull away. Marie bends over, her chin between her knees.

Sophia looks supplicating. She leans over, holds up a marker and stares at it. There is a single sentence as if on the shade, though we have none. Marie, wearing just a shirt, one knee against her chest, her other leg folded underneath her, is concentrated on the jar.

It was only a sentence formed of phrases left by a dream. Lewis lies on the bed, he takes off his glasses, he looks exhausted. His hand mentions me, he looks at me.

Marie makes a drawing of continuous circles, the floor is strewn with toys. The words are moving off like a line on the outside, it's just opinion like a vision, royally wide. I sit on the bed and for a moment I close my eyes. There's a butterfly behind me.

This is the introduction to love, she said the snow was a buffalo. I want to take a picture before the yellow willow but I could be seeing anything, not to despair. Marie says she's pretending to be a baby, she drops her sheet into the toilet. Sophia says something that sounds like what's this. The sentence was more like a meditation, it was nothing.

The dreams are so momentary, two weeks from now the whole story would be different but I can't say it would be a different story, I want to get high. Marie says she has both a penis and a vagina. She puts a ruler between her legs. She says this ruler is a hunt and it goes clap, it's summer and I'm hunting again. When I kiss her goodnight she says that was a hit-kiss.

The sentence was I don't want to stand around with you if you don't adore me. I read her a story. I'll stand, you lean your arm on my shoulder, full of camaraderie. Then you pull my hand down to feel your penis, it's not like the frost on the window which reminds me of the walls of the admiral's hut.

I sit with Marie listening to her be against sleep and then breathing sleep. I look at drawings of a lion and a peacock, a print of a woman, a poster of a tiger, a cardboard cutout of a peach. There's also a lemon and a turkey. I would have told you all those stories if you had been on my shoulder as you were or with me, that was why I wrote them down. Sometimes the story changes in remembering like the threat of extinction, shrinking forests, quarks, quasars and black holes, dirty snowballs and antirocks in space, I long for childhood to recite this introduction to love, it's so long.

Sophia's hands are covered with the colors of the markers. She cries when she's dressed, I wash her hands, you sing a song. You change her diaper, we're impatient, she drinks some juice. She says a word repeatedly that we don't understand. It takes so long and everyone tells me you're better off not eating the food you buy, each kind of food is tainted, then why do we husband it? Rosemary calls, she'll come on Sunday. Sophia goes to bed with her blanket and a meekness we all kiss.

It's been a mild winter, nothing to it, I have all the time in the world. I've forgotten where and who I am like fiction though winter's just beginning. It goes both fast and slow, my idea of it is lost like a movie seen for the second or third time. Not the winter, everything. I think sometimes no image is allowed but the image of love. Also no other noun. You're standing in the kitchen making coffee. Why is my civilized coat so dark and so little an answer to whether the rhythms of these words are sudden enough like American or too much so or moving? We are being quiet like the introduction to the opening theme at the beginning of the opera's overture, snow's coherence, nowhere to go, Sophia's not asleep yet. Could it be this whole thing is only about children? It surprises me when Marie still doesn't understand some thing, I've so assumed she is she like you. When will I begin? Now you know me, the children are Buddhas, I don't know why, I don't even like the idea. I'm lost because I can't stand on my head, I am writing you a letter, it begins,

Dear Lewis,

I know nothing is not an amazing thing to say, I do know nothing, I don't know what anything is, I'm lost among everything which is a green word and I know what everything is, loss of meaning, red and green, my compliments to you!

I am going to do something, a yellow word with some brown and green in the some and a main gray in the thing. Whatever I do I will have done it knowing nothing, that's all blue-gray among everything which is not always the same like the some of something.

Always has red in it and so does same, not so some. Red has green in it and only blue is blue. Orange has red in it, anyone will tell you that. I'm tired of being brilliant in this way like a tree. So were Mallarme and Rimbaud the lover of Verlaine whose name has all the colors. William Shakespeare has almost all the colors and so does Bernadette Mayer but I am a little bit darker. Clark Coolidge is predominantly tan and Lewis Warsh has many brownish-yellows and one primary, there is much charm in it and it isn't dark at all. Ted and Alice are different, Berrigan like Bernadette and Alice like the V of Verlaine or like alive. Each word leaps in this way. I dream I've forgotten all about it, then I myself leap up, What shall I do?

I'm not to do it yet but I do it already, I cannot not do it, I do it all the time, it's always the same thing, you see I see it all the time. There is a

beauty in description which comes before this
      detail as love
      I can't wait!
              "to make creation apter to perceive"
"I want to celebrate!"
            I know the rest of the night will be as devoted
to work as love as I'm now resting in this expensive sentence and in
the end I'll spend it fast writing to you anyway, addressing you and a
solution or night beginning like a letter, just a few words more freely
seeing everything more clearly than the rest of life and love tends to
be like windows facing mostly south but surrounding us, I'm think-
ing of you.

Falling down is a transition I offer you, I have a feeling I want to be
adored, is poetry a luxury, I won't defend it, I'll change my tone of
voice to share the rest but I won't end it. At the moment everything
seems to either fall down or stand up, leaves have fallen at least in the
past, no one gives credence to our lack of strategy and the placement
in an indefensible spot of our random-looking house like the price of
food or spices at the store though I don't defend eating like the truth
of pleasure told to one's mother.

Lentils, onions and potatoes are not expensive this year, carrots aren't
either. I can take it or leave it like the paper I write on lost like the
bottle with the note in the sea of what they call oceanic feelings, I'm
not romantic at all, I'm always scared of a fire, I'm as familiar as you
are with romantic love.

Listen, I had this idea, before I met you but after we kissed in the car
when I insisted on driving you right to the door though you said you
could easily walk, it was only around the block
      To someday become
      spendthrift of emotion
      as any girl or woman

No I don't mean that, I have this idea now to imitate you though I do
it in secret and attribute simple love to your idea of pleasure but be-

fore that I had an idea to write a book that would translate the detail of thought from a day to language like a dream transformed to read as it does, everything, a book that would end before it started in time to prove the day like the dream has everything in it, to do this without remembering like a dream inciting writing continuously for as long as you can stand up till you fall down like in a story to show and possess everything we know because having it all at once is performing a magical service for survival by the use of the mind like memory.

To be existing, to be existing and practicing as a poet, no I can't say that. In the past of the west and maybe further, poets told stories, they sang, they wrote epics, they composed for occasions. Inherent in the history of our lives together since I, all the while wanting to write this book, met you is a story, I don't know if I can tell it, I'll go as fast as I can on the occasion of this day.

Amidst the immodest disasters of our hooligan times, you were born to a composed family in the Bronx in 1944, no, I can't do it, it's too much like "This Is Your Life!" Remember the time you threw Anne and Kathy out of our house and I threw a bottle and broke the window, remember the feeling of being hemmed in by the snow, did I ever tell you about how Nick used to say if he saw two glasses on the table, who have you been sleeping with? David used to say if you could tell the story of exactly what is happening it would be amazing, but I can't do it, besides remembering is past approval even today I remember when Sophia was born and she lay on the bed before she made a sound like a warrior sprung from the ground or Athena from the head of Zeus, we did dance you and I and go to anybody's parties, we would celebrate, we would be inside this house of not remembering, we would be shocked as innocence remembers where we used to sleep, we would gradually give night's recuperating balance to the day, not ever trusting to have enough time, we would obsessively count kinds of days, one of us would remember another version of a story about the other, we would sleep and dream we're only inside this or that house, it would have an extra room this time, we would dream the same or a complementary thing, we'd wonder about this isolation, we would eventually begin

to dance with our daughters, we would change to become less lost to
the rest we hadn't seen for all love's blinding we would still lose noth-
ing, it's in the ribbons of her hair.

> So when I write of love I write of
> Binding referendums, bankruptcy intent,
> Industrials, utilities and sales
> The petitions of a citizens' group
> Transportation, births, corrections,
> The downtown mall, the toy fund,
> The predictions of the meteorologist,
> Hearing-aid discounts, oil-price increases,
> Ice fishing, diplomatic ties with China,
> An exploding oil depot in Rhodesia,
> A controversial nuclear physicist,
> South Africa's resources of chrome
> And Russia's stores of platinum and tin,
> Intercontinental ballistic missiles,
> Mexican oil, student assemblies,
> Mobile homes uprooted by strong winds,
> Book sales, Chris Evert's engagement,
> The uses of trees on the banks of reservoirs,
> The victory of the Cleveland Cavaliers
> And how the Sabres beat the Flames,
> I write of artists, auto technicians,
> Babysitters, bookkeepers, child care workers,
> Companions, conference managers, cooks,
> Dental assistants and receptionists,
> Designers, electricians, English teachers,
> Hairdressers, maintenance men and women,
> Medical secretaries, mold makers, night clerks,
> Nurses, oil-burner-service technicians,
> Program directors, programmer trainees,
> Public health nurses, registered nurses,
> Secretaries, ski salesmen and saleswomen,

Substitute teachers, waitresses and waiters,
I write of bribery and surgery,
Changes in the sentencing of criminals,
A plan to change garbage to industrial steam,
The Pope's speech about his first trip,
Jet hijackings, price rises, a recession,
The People's Temple hit list, the findings
Of the House Assassinations Committee
A high-level mission to Taipei, Taiwan,
New Federal oil-industry regulations,
Freed North Korean political prisoners,
The Strategic Arms Limitation Treaty,
The tree warden, the wind storm, the ice,
A selectmen's meeting, disco dancers,
A recipe for a pineapple coffee wreath,
A consultant to a toy manufacturer,
Victorian dollhouses, the art of woodcarvers,
The extradition of a former FBI spy,
A Colombian novelist's human rights group,
A singing ferry, red and silver foxes,
Drugs to lower the level of cholesterol,
Discrepancies in reports of a midair crash,
Marriages, inquiries, public notices,
The financial default of the city of Cleveland,
Inflation, the OTB simulcast bid,
The defeat of the Knicks by the Hawks,
Army allegedly breaking recruiting rules,
The Nets' loss to the Rockets,
King's arrest for drunk driving and cocaine,
Rick Barry's outburst of anger at the fans,
Minimum wages, apartheid, the United Nations,
Inflation, widespread default on bank loans,
The fight at the meeting of the women's bank,
The gasoline tax plan, Dictaphone stock gains,
The merger of Continental Phone with Executone,
Napoleons, eclairs, tarts and tortes,

Reborn Christians, women in the Jaycees,
The Council on Aging, protesting teachers,
A nuclear power plant, high school violence,
The inventor of earmuffs, free ski lessons,
Speeding, drunken driving and accidental deaths,
Carolers, a graphics firm, window paintings,
Air-pollution emission, foreclosures,
A report of missing gold, gangs, crashes,
Frauds, bombed buildings, the crisis in Iran,
Information from the surface of Venus,
A bus hit by a train, remade movies,
A papal message censored in Poland,
The murder of a Basque militant leader,
Collages, operas, stages, the soft shoe,
Romantic films, the writers of "Superman,"
Clint Eastwood with a monkey, bad plots,
Old jazz musicians, Russian body mime,
Two Soviet films, expensive restaurants,
RKO, MGM, progressive rock experimentation,
Japanese architecture, chamber music,
Auctions, Andy Warhol and Red Grooms,
A lost anarchist novelist, contract bridge,
Biographies, the Bible, documentaries,
Cosmology and the Balinese dance,

                                        Bernadette.

I write this love as all transition
As if I'm in instinctual flight
                              a small lady bug
With only two black dots on its back
Climbs like a blind turtle on my pen
And begins to drink ink in the light
                                   of tradition
We're allowed to crowd love in
Like a significant myth
                           resting still on paper
I remember being bitten by a spider

92

It was like feeling what they call
                    the life of the mind
Stinging my thigh like Dante
                    this guilty beetle
Is a frightening thing
When it shows its wings
And leaps like the story of a woman who
                              once in this house
Said the world was like a madhouse
                         cold winds blowing
And life looks like some malignant disease,
Viewed from the heights of reason
Which I don't believe in
                    I know the place
Taken by tradition is like superstition
And even what they call the
Literary leaves less for love
                    I know
The world is straight ice
I know backwards the grief of life like chance
                                   if I can say that
I can say easily I know you
                    like the progression
From memory to what they call freedom
Or reason
         though it's not reason at all
It's an ideal like anarchism though it's not an ideal
It's a kind of time that has flown away from causes
Or gotten loose from them, pried loose
Or used them up, gotten away
                         no one knows why
Nothing happens
There is no reason, there's no dream
                              it's not inherited
Like peace but it's not peace
                         there's no beginning
Like religion but it is not God

It's more like middle age or humor
Without elucidation
                like greeting-card verse
This love is a recognized occasion
I know you like I know my times
As if I were God and gave you birth
                        if I can say that
I can say I am Ra who drew from himself
To give birth to Geb and Nut, Isis and Osiris
Though it isn't decorous today to say this
                       instead I say
You are the resource for my sense of decorum
Knowing you as Ra knew the great of magic,
His imaginary wife,
             and without recourse to love
Men and women are like tears
               I would lose my memory,
I would sleep twelve hours, I would wake up
And get into my boat with my scribe,
I would study the twelve hours of the day
Spending an hour in each
             I would have a secret name
I would rush upon the guilty without pity
Till the goddess of my eye in her vengeance
Overwhelmed my own rage
            as you and I take turns
In love's anger like the royal children
Born every morning to die that night
             I know you speak
And are as suddenly forgiven,
It's the consequence of love's having no cause
Then we wonder what we can say
            I can say
I turn formally to love to spend the day,
To you to form the night as what I know,
An image of love allows what I can't say,
Sun's lost in the window and love is below

Love is the same and does not keep that name
I keep that name and I am not the same
A shadow of ice exchanges the color of light,
Love's figure to begin the absent night.

• PART SIX •

In Yokuntown we write all night
In the literal, love and experimental ways
I've met alot of people who think I should write novels
I wonder what I'll look like when I'm old
We put the food away
                              I lie down and think
How we still need diapers and beer
I begin to dream I'm an undertaker
                                        there are numerous funerals,
A wriggler is the larva of a mosquito, there's
A person who cannot write,
                              a point on a map or diagram,
A symbol for a kiss or kisses in letters,
The roman numeral ten, it's Xmas again,
Two black undertakers I see close up
Wait for me to follow them like Christ,
A person or thing unrevealed,
                              xenon,
A sign of multiplication, an abscissa,

                                I see Rita,
I see all the young poets in a room with me
They're drinking all the beer
There's only apple juice left, Gerard's gotten fat
I don't undertake to understand it
                             Then I meet Ed
He says he had the same dream as I did
He's seen the same undertakers
X marks the spot
                    This morning Lewis dreamed
He was going to San Francisco, California
On a train all alone
                      I dream I'm on a train
That's not on its tracks, it's askew
I drop a burning cigarette ash on the steps
Of an indoor fire escape
And when I try to stamp it out
The whole escape flies away
From the building it's attached to
                          I'd better call
Mr. Hatch and get it all fixed
                            I meet a woman who says
"Do you want some feedback on your meal?"
I've got stockings on like the ones Ray gave me
She hoped I wouldn't mind they were hers
                              They get stuck
In some machine which is functioning
Under the table
                Then another woman
Gets me some other ones
Real inflatable nylon stockings
From the People's Republic of China
Like the new soy sauce we bought, Superior Soy
                                I'm a boy again
I follow two men into the subway
                        It's the undertakers
I shout to them to wait, wait for me

                                Then I remember
One of them is just an ember
He's a man who's already dead
                                like the need
To know what's going on in the world
But not so much you forget where you are
Like a fiction or religion or a wholesale agitator
                                                    I wake up
Less rested than relieved
I'll never have to undertake to go through that again
I hate dates and their significance in death's memories,
Arbitrary yearly meetings with pre-Xmas dreams
                                                    In life

I call up Peggy, it's her birthday
And she's had a bad dream
She's depressed about the holidays
And can't remember anything
We have an enlivening talk about craving sleep
And the clues in our dreams full of mothers and fathers
We feel better, we'll get together
For the New Year up here
                                What is reading and writing
I have to go to the cold grocery store
It's an icy night, the nicest man in town says
Have a nice weekend
                        At the package store
Young Mr. Wheeler is talking to a woman who says
"I'm past the child-bearing age," then she says
"Just like my washing machine . . ."
She looks young to me and not like a machine
                                                    I see
One of the hairdressers getting into his
American sportscar
                        he says,
"Getting ready for the holidays?"
Desultorily I say I see what you mean
                                        I slip on the ice

Ice on the trees is lit by streetlights
There's no moon yet, I slip because I'm racing
By now for fear, will I ever get home?
What is reading and writing,
This pledge to get to the desk which opens,
It's a piece of wood like a boat
Carved and cut and hinged and screwed
To hold up the weight of my hands and arms,
The typewriter and the beer, I have a mirror,
I'm between two windows which makes it so cold
I have to wear a down vest when I write,
I'm lucky to have one
                                    Wagner felt he had to wear
Satin dressing gowns in order to compose
I am ashamed that death obsesses me
But death is just the usual
The obsessiveness is something I won at poker
Where I'm remembering what's been played
So I can play my hand so no one ever dies
                                         How preoccupying
Is the wish to include all or to leave all out
Some say either wish is against a poem or art
                                    I'm asking
Is it an insane wish?
                         To be beseiged, beset with,
To have to sit with, to be harassed, obsessed,
To be possessed or ruled by
                              I am confused by
Fear, perfection and love, this poem,
Order, mourning, vigilance and beer
And cigarettes and directness
Or clarity, words, truth or writing
Or the sublime
                  Everyday
These apologies are what they call under control
I've no respect for their repetitious logic
And though I'm obsessed with keeping track

Of where you are in the house or out of it
I rarely clean it thoroughly
                              having gotten older
I'm obseesed with how I look but
I don't pay attention to it either
                              The structure
Of the past has always given me the feeling
That as long as things are okay
There's a rhythm to that which chances are
Won't be broken
                    But once something awful happens
Then you're in for it as it doesn't fit
That's why I like recovering
And am always doing it but
When I think each time I write a line
I know someone I know won't approve of it
I begin to wonder about my mother
                                My mother thought
It was opals that brought
Bad luck, many people then used to say
People die in three's
                    My mother said
Even if you try to get rid of an opal
It will bring you trouble
                    Lucky Chaucer said
I have great wonder, be this light
How I can live . . .
                    I was going to tell about garbage
And how taking it down to the yard
Ought to be a lucky pleasure at least compared
To any other place I've taken garbage down to
But like recovering from an illness or grief
And rejoicing for a while in a new ordinary way of being
And then forgetting you were ever sick or aggrieved,
Pleasure without any change becomes a chore
Though in some old-hat division of labor
                                to change the subject

Lewis has become so good at dealing with it
                                I mean the garbage
And I do cook the dinners
                        But what I meant to say was
Just the way it's impressive and new
To visit friends who surprise you
By being attentive and fastidious
To one thing and not another and I wish
Then to imitate them for a while
Because it seems there might be something to it,
So I wish I was more like the young woman
The papers said today was confused
                                She hijacked a plane
In an attempt to free the same prisoner
Her mother was killed trying to free
In another hijacking
                I guess I'm already a little like her
The papers said the prisoner was her mother's lover
And he'd convinced the girl he was her father
Though she had no way of knowing
                                In the hijacking
She became exhausted and lost her stubborn will
To keep the passengers prisoner on the plane
And when she was arrested in what the papers called
Her alleged attempt, she was alone and
There's a picture of the girl on the arms of the police
Before the cold Illinois photographers,
She's put a coat over her head
                                Now it's inevitable
She'll go to prison but for a plea
That a person as young as she
With all the confusion in her life
Had no idea what she was doing
                                So animistically
I wonder sometimes if what I've got tied to my back
Is more like her harmless railroad flares than this anger

Of the explosion of real dynamite which might endanger
Others, the innocent others who are always standing around
What in fact are they doing? Aren't they thinking
Enough not to be in the vicinity of a misled killer-to-be
Like you or me, what does it look like?
                                        Lately Lewis and I
Have been running out of matches
In Massachusetts it's legal to buy
                                strike anywhere's
I'm exhausted as the girl who is not a myth
I ask Lewis for the matches and he says he ate them
Like a hungry Iranian demonstrator on the Teheran streets
Shouting "Death to the Shah!"
                                David once convinced me
I thought I had eaten my parents
                                To add insult to injury
Is a phrase that has always interested me
                                        So I might say
When my mother got sick with the disease
From which she died she said
It was probably all our fault
Because in what they call in court
Our attempt to love we had in fact punched her
I read some old writer who says to learn about life
You have to be in court or in camp
                                this is what obsessions are
For anyone who doesn't already know what it means
When you wash your hands
You still have yet to wash what you touched
While you were beginning to wash them
And in the end there's no end but forgetting
Or to die in a frenzy of unremitting love
                                        or take heroin
Or keep a stash of it for dying
Like the Antarctic explorers or like double agents in movies
Or even plain soldiers or emotion's jaded hijackers

Though freezing to death is said to be euphoric
And Scott wrote twelve letters while he died at the Pole
But not like the people in Guyana
Who died of cyanide in Kool-Aid in bubonic-plague-
Type contortions on the bodies of their children
                                        Wait!
I thought I was going to talk about reading and writing
And not the desire to renew love to life
In proportion to obsession by endless fucking
                                        To reveal
In Yokuntown we write all night
Not that it's natural or even known about
                                        Just to fill up
Some space as existence is generous and frenzied
And to alight in a certain spot outside,
                                to write

Like a bird migrating or returning
This town is now a feeding station
As it once was just a tavern or an inn
On the road between two places more well known
Now the space is filled, what of overpopulation?
We don't pretend to die but we write invisibly
Hoarding our time and cherishing our family
We don't even want to be famous but we do
                                hope to survive
We meet in the hallway which becomes the road
Between the rooms in which we write
We publish books and a magazine,
                        United Artists,
We sell our letters, we apply for grants
                        Lewis' parents
Send us a hundred fifty dollars every month
Which is enough for food
                        Writing is a need
And when there's time a pleasure
                        Living together
On the schedules of babies in the country's luxury

Our lives are circumscribed, we lack distractions
At random we have visitors, usually all at once
Some people don't seem to like the children
And when they come to see us they ignore them
As if the sentient children were as unintentional
As our presence in ironic New England
                                        Some say
This place is too pretty or too clean, not Marxist
Or Leninist or Maoist enough,
                            why live anywhere?
Some people must live somewhere
Or cannot or do not want to move,
Everywhere there is has everything there is to look at,
Some are even afraid to move
                            I understand that
Perhaps I've thought a bit too much about it
It's San Francisco I always thought was too pretty
But not these small cold hills
                        Often someone walks in the door
And the first thing they say is why do you live here
Among these tight-assed Yankees in the cold
                                    I say
It's best it's me who does
I'm just as close-mouthed, secretive and stodgy
As any Yankee in my way, I love to work and pay
The hideous price of seeking infinite knowledge
In this orphaned place with its changing light,
Pure air, temperate extremes of weather's drama,
Beauty of the self-denial hills and sybarite trees,
Marshes, bogs, swamps, rocks, caves and small towns,
Scenes of glacial happenings, still part of the world
Everywhere a somewhat like expression as far as I can see
Though I'm not the type who minds the cold
                                        and in the past
I've been told I'm just as cold and in winter dark
And unchanging as these coldly charming hills
Whose visages alarmed Nathaniel Hawthorne, a man,

If we endeavor to speak thus, as nervous as I

                                       Jesus!

I don't mind the beauty of it all at all

                              Some say

The life we have is wrong because we've been lucky

And don't work in a factory or at a CETA job

But it's petty to spend poetry complaining

Unless I were a pilgrim in *The Canterbury Tales*

And then I could say anything

                        So just because we're married

Don't dismiss us, don't forget to include us

In all the gay anthologies as a family

                           We are still crazy

And repentant and rushing the gorgeous past

As the ice creeps into the house

                      If again I've said too much

Maybe the rest is as if it were simple

But I can't defend our hearts tongue in cheek

As if they were recalcitrant to love

And we'd already begun to look alike

                        We always were

As we've become, alternating in our habits

At once rushing to be loved ridiculously freely

At once hiding the place of love in the closet

The doors of which are never closed

So the children call it the airport

                      As coincidences,

Simple complications, decorum and the order of meetings

Astound us more up or over here

                      Is all this too abstract

Just to clear some space as if in the kitchen

And not really clean?

                Is loving to be outside

The same as love, just walking and inheriting

Plain movement from relative time

                     which is accurate

Unlike volume and distance

For measuring even love
The way something in the distance
Stays the same and you might say
Those clouds are chasing me?
                        It might not prevent me
From ceasing to love only you
                        Love prevents my knowing
Some loves are overwhelming
Like the unknown but fashionable perfection
Of an atomic clock
                    I say there is nothing
Even a small town
With nothing in it
& nobody to talk to
To stop me loving you, a song
                        I am bewildered then
By death, we all read all about it like fear
As if every day we make sure like another
To put in time being crazy for fear
                        we will not ever die,
We won't lose our touch for death
And every time I think I've got it down
I learn I'm not for death at all
                        I am depressed like a plant
By midwinter's intransigence as if it were a baby
Without any enlightening daring or soft skin
                            I know the purpose
Of human stubbornness because I know the person
But what's this unemotional drastic nature of the place?
The only answer I can think of is I know
I didn't have to learn to love you
                        So I only see
The headless winter as a spectacular
Or boring thing
                    Not like saying "Fuck you!" in rage,
The fallen tree no analogy to age or disease,
But all as explicit surprise and if you knew all about it

You'd find in your emotion to excite plain seeing
You had probably left out the most important part,
Mistaking the sights for an audience
                                    I think I know the trees
Will never love me and we're here as accidentally
To eat, sleep and work in an ordinary way,
To be astonished by will as time is slow to be
Amazed by speed and pleasure, frantic natures
As fast and reactionary as writing in lines
                                    to learn
What I once began to do and then left off
Like a baby's talent for walking at birth
                                    I still try to go too fast
As if the press of everything were identical,
I type up a poem and head for home
Clear letters on androgynous paper
I sit at the family table where it's a struggle
To create both staminate and pistillate in the same
Inflorescence of cluster, I feel a great impatience,
All the people in my family have sensuous lips
I say like a man or woman who does head home
With all that dirt under my nails
                                    I know nothing
But the lassitude of love
                                    Half an hour after sunset
All the windows are frozen shut
                                    Like psychology
I have to hammer the sides with my fists
To get them to open, often I wonder
If I think the same things I thought as a child
When I didn't know the future of a form
                                    Now I look different
For a woman to look different is still more difficult,
Though each moving being who changes thinks,
Than for the man of the tribe
                                    A tribe is one of three
From the Latin into which the Romans

Were originally divided,
                          Latin, Sabine, Etruscan,
And the tribe together with
Families, slaves and adopted strangers meant
A recognized community plus a form of the future
                                        to become
Like the phylae of ancient Greece
Or the twelve divisions of the Israelites
Or any group of people or animals or plants
With some of the same habits and ideas
                                  like the futures
Of the women who may think they've lost their charms
Or the men who think they've changed
                                beyond recognition
Like a community or a person who thinks
If only we could all get some sleep
                          like Chaucer
Or a Latin Sabine or Etruscan mother
Who didn't have the time, chance, education or notion
To write some poetry so I could know
What she thought about things
                          There are some who did anyway,
There's Anne Bradstreet and Tsai Wen Gi,
Elizabeth Barrett Browning, Alice Notley and me,
Adrienne Rich, Sylvia Plath, Anne Sexton,
Elinor Wylie, Louise Bogan, Denise Levertov,
There's Barbara Guest, H.D. and Harriet Beecher Stowe,
Maureen Owen, Nikki Giovanni, Diane di Prima,
Murasaki Shikibu, Fanny Howe and Susan Howe,
Muriel Rukeyser, Mina Loy, Lorine Neidecker,
Gwendolyn Brooks, Marina Tsvetayeva and Anna Akhmatova,
There's Rebecca Wright
And the saints
            I read in the papers that women live longer
Because they don't do all of this
And as they begin to become more like men
In all these ways they'll die equally soon

I forgot to mention

George Sand,

As if death were not life

and I was dressed as a man

Racing around as a woman among a race of women

Too relegated before to birth like Mary Shelley

And a division of labor into whatever it was or is

To write a secret history,

for desire to be like food

Touching history with desire

For history to be like food

On the table in the light of the window

It's shared

There are some things we cannot say!

No, I can't say that!

The awful presence of the obvious,

abdicated time,

Never relents in its demand to speak all at once

Because but for that there's the chance

The rest of what's begun to be lost might be lost

Like putting all one's bushels in an apple forever

Like the story changed or forgotten to make

A priestly transformation in the lives of the people

And in their words

Like an ordinance imposed

In proud moments by the tellers of tales

Or by politicians to a purpose

This present future,

Old as it is, is an inaccessible time

Where idiosyncratic western women,

most from what they call

The privileged classes,

but not only those,

Are beginning to write enough so that everyone

Can find a chair in heaven

I say he or she

Even in history, probably never knew before

Who's crying
                It's a parliament of women, I won't mention
The prices of spices because talents are equal
To inheritance and love
                  following the rules
But still the stunning stone of a girl is less carved,
There's no way around it
                  not that life is any wilder
Let loose from a woman than from a man
We are all descendants of sexes as in varying clothing
Nor is the admonition of form ever less
Than the loving constrictions of the great ones
Of any kind of health, class or time
                  After all writing
And the genius of poetry only holds up half the sky
Like a woman born to a social occasion
Become a battle or a war for change
                  like Freud and Sappho
You sent me a meal once in this pot I still have
Where, in among that, I can only be as great
As Shakespeare or Milton or Chaucer or Dante
Or any of the others
I have the pleasure
Of knowing all about
                  But the meal I mentioned
Which had only been
Pot roast with gravy and potatoes
Not less remembered
Is worshipped and defended
                  whenever I see
Men in trees
And I want to be a worker in trees,
Winter-long I would paint the city if I see a cityscape,
And from what I saw I even want to be involved
In photo realist painting, airbrush painting,
Pattern painting and proposals for sculptures,
Performances, photos and texts, color field painting,

New image painting, silkscreen collage and watercolors,
Monoprints, landscapes, lithographs, etchings,
Body art, silverpoint, pop art, op art, nudes,
California funk art, frescoes, floor sculpture,
All kinds of wallpieces and shaped canvasses,
Outdoor projects, snow sculptures and still lifes,
Architectural drawings and post-minimalist sculpture,
Sky sculpture, all kinds of oil and figure painting,
Wood block prints, murals, bronzes and monuments,
Tapestries, mobiles, seascapes, poster art and films,
Minimal painting, precisionist painting, formalist painting,
New realist painting, minimal sculpture, abstract expressionism,
Even video art, narrative art, paper reliefs and aquatints,
Flower painting, wood carvings, sketches and calligraphy,
Egg tempera paintings, graffiti and all of photography,
Process art, grid paintings, stripe paintings, light art,
Happenings, kinetic sculpture, environmental sculpture
And pastels, ceramics, multimedia presentations, portraits,
Social realism and collages
                                    I would even discover roughly
Adrenalin, air conditioning, a satellite of Pluto,
Supermassive objects in the centers of galaxies,
The airplane, the jet propulsion airplane, helicopters,
Mass spectography of stable isotopes, penicillin,
Insulin and its production by bacteria, antimatter,
The depths that fish inhabit, the Polaroid Land camera,
The all-electronic numerical integrator and calculator,
The digital computer, cloning, the cultivation of truffles,
The conditioned reflex, the cyclotron, the neon lamp,
Deuterium, celanese fibers, polyesters and polyamides,
The double-helical structure of DNA, the tungsten filament,
The equivalence of mass and energy, the mercury vapor lamp,
Nylon, "heat death," recombinant DNA techniques, the laser
The stored-program computer concept, test-tube babies,
Antiviral drugs, restriction enzymes, paper and the loom,
Neutron-induced radiation, nuclear fission, the ball-point,

Cosmetics, the crossbow, a drop in the sun's temperature,
The first gamma ray spectral line, the rings of Uranus,
Sulfur ions around Jupiter, a mouse with a human chromosome,
A mouse derived from six parents, radar, nuclear reactors,
The vacuum electron tube, sound motion pictures, protons,
Positrons, polio vaccine, gunpowder and the forked plow,
The rotary internal comustion engine, the gyrocompass,
Intelligence testing, natural satellites of asteroids,
A cure for traveler's diarrhea, the automatic rifle,
Psychoanalysis, the special and general theories of relativity,
Alpha and beta particle radiation, gamma radiation, vitamins,
Color film with three emulsion layers, electron microscopes,
Geometry, synthetic plastic, the polymerization process,
Quantum theory, the Wassermann test, the flush toilet,
Solar-weather links, a pocket-size three-dimensional camera,
Sulfa drugs, military tanks, tractors, transistors, t.v.'s,
The uncertainty principle, the Van Allen radiation belt,
Zero, the wheel, Lucifer yellow, charm quarks and supernova,
An end to locust plagues, the reason for the "East Coast booms,"
The synthesis of the transuranic elements including Fermium,
Americium, Einsteinium, Curium, Berkelium and Californium,
Animal prescience of earthquakes, gravity waves, antiprotons,
The nature of schizophrenia and the first known noon marker
Of the summer solstice
                           I would close my red eyes like copper
And watch you by the atomic clock
To have the luxury to love at least in theory
Indivisibly for a time in the sweetest exchanges
As if the world were not enraged,
                           You go out for cigarettes,
As if love is not the food
Of those of us satisfied enough to write
To write to lend urgency pleasure, to sing,
To celebrate, to inspire, to reveal
                           You put on
Your gotten shoes and coat in an image

And say you will be right back
                              While you're out love is stored
In intensest house, this cave of it,
                              We go too fast,
Switched from the speed of variegated love
Writing's married and fallen in with family,
Though it's more exhausting to love to write
Than to pursue what might have been described
About the past as being fast,
                              Sometimes we feel like
Fools, lunatics, paranoid hermits having manic flights
With nothing coming of it
                              No invitations to cocktails or tea
With the whole American Indian nation,
No requests to write a column for The Post,
                              no demands for words
For occasions, for public celebrations or for mourning,
For invocations for grace for change
                              But each night
Craving any sweet joy
We still hope to live a long time
                              Hurry you say
And we love to hurry
But not to speed up the night
                              To be rushed to be kissed
To be irrationally married to words and produce
Wildness like a child or two, not grown up yet,
Perfection, a genius, not going as fast
As the speed of the past again where everyone
Is thought to be another to this day
                              like a letter
We never forget about
We run from place to place to answer it
                              Love is coveted
We have no need of the commandments
Alone in the house among the secrets
. We still work to tell

Without pause there is a purpose,
Anyone does it who is knowing all about it
How far can I go with it getting away with it
Before I die the fool and if I die will I
Have missed something and am I always the same
Though now I'm two or even four I wish to be more
I don't know why, I know I don't like to buy

                                    Xmas presents
But if I had some money today I'd buy love's surprises
And present them to the people on my list, they are
Lewis, Ray, Harry, Sophia and Marie all the Warshes,
Rosemary Mayer, Margaret DeCoursey, Grace Murphy,
Alice Notley, Ted and Anselm and Edmund Berrigan,
Raphael Soyer, Lynn O'Hare and Moses and Bill Berkson,
Bill, Beverly, Marnie and Arden Corbett, Simon Schuchat,
Clark, Celia and Susan Coolidge, Paul and Nancy Metcalf,
Bob and Eileen Callahan, Bill Kushner, Charlotte Carter,
Bob and Ali Rosenthal and Rochelle Kraut, John Ensslin,
Ed Friedman, Kenward Elmslie, Susan Noel, Meg Simon,
Joe Brainard, Rudy Burckhardt, Ed & Tom Bowes and Harris,
And Charlie Vermont whose 33rd birthday it is
And many other people I've seen and known,
Now Lewis has come home

                          I thought I was going to write
A story of my theories tonight
Not this desirous essay on art and home,
This alarming dictionary of reformist love

                                    Is it safe
To say that, knowing my notebook?

                              The moon is coming up
I have something to do with that

                              Tonight the Shah of Iran
Is not watching his forty-inch t.v. and what might be
The dread implications of overwhelming power has become
A confusion of the magic wishes of everyone
And the titillating knowledge of almost everything
Lost before in the complicated stories of dreams

Where the moment is supreme so joint with the past
Found in awakening to love of rearranging
This world at best at random translated
                                    By the eyes of ice
To a detail of truth,
                        Something is discovered,
We wait to see what happens
We hope it's not a war or suffering
And that the women will shake off the veil
In the myriad future of our still
Revolutionary munificent dreams, our lust
For surprise benefitting us like the sun
Like the supplicating weather we fear
May suddenly change from what it is
To another ice age but not before
The climate warms undetectably
Forcing us all to move to the moon
                                There we gather
Supplies in airtight containers,
                            force ideas
From dreams to develop the craft of sleep,
Keep in touch with what's happening,
                                wonder
At nature, emergencies, extreme heat,
Cold and unassailably new beauty,
                                births,
Unusual time exposures of the earth,
Intercourse, sex, copulation, fucking,
I think I wrote this in the dark
                        There's a light
In my eyes afterwards by chance
Like a family
                That dumb streetlight like the moon
Shines in my one window out of nine in the house
With its green white-town pinkish light
Rich in ultraviolet and actinic rays

And with my eyes
I'm reading a paper on us fucking in mercury vapor
I found I was finding another position
                                        for the diaphragm
Like the curtain like the moon's oval pebbles
Under the exciting microscope
Of the Western world
                        I speak out loud against it
Other lights in the town might be broken
By accident or widespread vandalism
But they're too high and look like Christ
On the cross with the hands of an eye's fluorescent fish
Like a talent unspotlit and queer
                                        To be me is to be
Queer sleep after death, its modesty deriving
What from the eyes of the immodest living
Is offered at the cost of a ruinous leaving
Well, I have to close them
                                This paid incandescent light
Is like the vigil of a virgin
Last to tell before my eyes I'll end.

From dreams I made sentences, then what I've seen today,
Then past the past of afternoons of stories like memory
To seeing as a plain introduction to modes of love and reason,
Then to end I guess with love, a method to this winter season
Now I've said this love it's all I can remember
Of Midwinter Day the twenty-second of December

Welcome sun, at last with thy softer light
That takes the bite from winter weather
And weaves the random cloth of life together
And drives away the long black night!